CONTENTS

3	Architectural Beginnings
7	Introduction
13	Department of Education Building
17	Transport House
19	BMA House
21	City Mutual Life Building
25	Sydney Morning Herald Building
29	Bryant House
33	Commonwealth Bank Building
37	MLC Building
41	Sun Building
43	David Jones Buildings
47	Hyde Park Anzac Memorial
51	Foys Building
55	Plaza Theatre
59	Metropolitan Water, Sewerage & Drainage Board Building
61	Gowings Building
65	Dymocks Building
69	Grace Building
73	AWA Tower
77	Railway House
79	Commercial Banking & Bank of NSW Buildings
83	Sydney Harbour Bridge
86	George Raynor Hoff
88	Timeline
90	Glossary

N

W

E

S

ARCHITECTURAL BEGINNINGS

When Captain Arthur Phillip sailed into Botany Bay, on the east coast of Australia, in January 1788, he was unimpressed. The bay was unprotected and shallow and surrounded by poor soil and its shore was observed to be unproductive with scarce fresh water. Having led a fleet of ships halfway around the world to found a penal colony for British convicts, he decided to explore further north for a better location.

He found it just 12 kilometres up the coast. Port Jackson was an inlet discovered and named by Captain James Cook in 1770 although it was not extensively explored at the time. What Phillip found as he ventured up the inlet was, in his opinion, 'the finest harbour in the world'.

Named after the British Home Secretary Thomas Townshend (Lord Sydney), Sydney Cove was a well sheltered deep water anchorage with ample fresh water supplies. It was a perfect site for the first official British settlement on the Australian continent.

FOR THE FIRST TWO DECADES OF SYDNEY'S EXISTENCE THE COLONY WAS SO LACKING IN APPROPRIATE SKILLS AND TOOLS THAT THE MAJORITY OF BUILDINGS CONSTRUCTED WERE OF POOR QUALITY AND IN NEED OF CONSTANT MAINTENANCE.

The situation changed dramatically with the appointment of Major-General Lachlan Macquarie as Governor of New South Wales in 1810. Finding many structures throughout the settlement in a 'most ruinous state of decay', Macquarie implemented a set of building codes that dictated a minimum standard for any future construction. Teaming up with convicted forger and architect Francis Greenway, the Governor also commissioned a series of classically inspired public buildings including Hyde Park Barracks (1819) and St James Church (1824), both of which still stand today.

From the mid to late 19th century architectural trends in Sydney closely followed those adopted throughout the British Empire. Grand classical revival styles were used extensively for public and administrative buildings whilst well to do residents displayed their wealth with elaborate Victorian Italianate or sober Georgian home designs.

6

INTRODUCTION

The dawn of the 20th century signalled a series of significant changes to the social and urban fabric of Australia. The year 1901 saw the death of Queen Victoria (along with her eponymous 19th century era) after a reign of 63 years, and witnessed the birth of the nation of Australia with the federation of the colonies. Sydney became the capital of the state of New South Wales with a turn of the century population of around 480,000, making it one of the largest cities in the Western world.

Architecturally, styles popular in the late 1800s continued to be utilised for new buildings throughout the city, occasionally incorporating design elements from contemporary trends emerging from Europe such as the Art Nouveau movement. 'Federation' is the umbrella term, coined in 1969, that covers the period from around 1890 to 1915 and encompasses such revival styles as Free Classical, Anglo-Dutch and Queen Anne.

DESPITE FORMING A NEW NATION AT THE BEGINNING OF A NEW CENTURY, AS WITH THE PREVALENT ARCHITECTURAL STYLES, THERE WAS A LINGERING DESIRE TO MAINTAIN STRONG TIES TO THE OLD WORLD.

Australia felt obliged to maintain the prestige of the British Empire and when war erupted in 1914 Australian sons rushed to defend it. Four years later Europe was in ruins and millions of lives had been lost, including over 60,000 Australians. The war had deeply shocked the nation but its end triggered a building boom to provide housing for returned soldiers and their families. In Sydney a general economic upturn and increasing prosperity in the immediate post-war years also led to major redevelopments and construction in the CBD. In addition to architectural styles such as Art Deco and early Modernism, new building technologies were adopted from the United States enabling the design of taller buildings and apartments.

Although the Great Depression slowed or halted much of this new urban development throughout the 1930s, it also produced one of Sydney's most impressive and recognisable feats of civil engineering, the Sydney Harbour Bridge.

Overall the inter-war years saw the modernisation of Sydney, transforming a low rise 19th century city into an increasingly high rise 20th century metropolis.

11

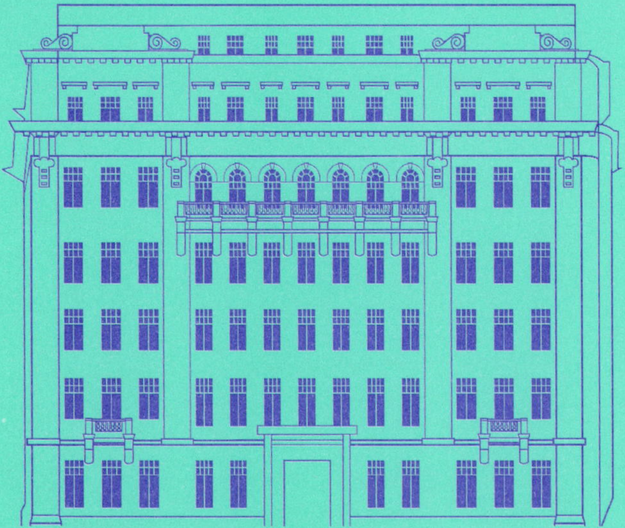

1 35 Bridge St / 1914 / George McRae

DEPARTMENT OF EDUCATION BUILDING

Occupying an entire city block, the imposing Department of Education Building was one of the last stone-faced structures to be commissioned by the NSW Government. George McRae was a Scottish architect who, having migrated to Australia in 1884, was appointed City Architect in 1889. Over the following years he designed many of Sydney's grandest architectural landmarks including the Queen Victoria Building (1898), becoming New South Wales Government Architect in 1912. McCrae's later projects were primarily designed in the Edwardian Baroque style (later termed Federation Free style), reflecting contemporary architectural fashions in England, and this building is a particularly handsome example.

Sitting on a rusticated sandstone base the first level features articulated quoins and piers. A pattern of symmetrically placed rectangular windows and balcony arrangements is repeated on each elevation with a series of arched openings decorating the upper levels. The top floor is capped with a relatively simple cornice with dentils, above which rises the roof parapet. The Bridge Street facade is entered via a central porch flanked by Doric columns and topped by an ornately decorated broken pediment. The seamless unified appearance of the building belies the fact that it was actually built in two stages. The north section was constructed c1912-14 whilst the southern part was added in 1930.

✪ OF NOTE

Booth House / 1938 / 44 Bridge Street

Opposite the Department of Education Building, on the corner of Bridge and Young Streets, is the former 'Booth House', named after the original owners Frederick H. Booth & Sons. A fine example of the Late Deco Functionalist style, bands of brick divide large ribbon windows that allow maximum light to penetrate the office spaces. Unusually for a progressive inter-war building, the base is composed of rusticated sandstone.

Although the decorative features and heavy masonry facades recall 19th century architectural styles, the building was constructed using contemporary steel frame and concrete slab methods, demonstrating the emerging technology of the new century.

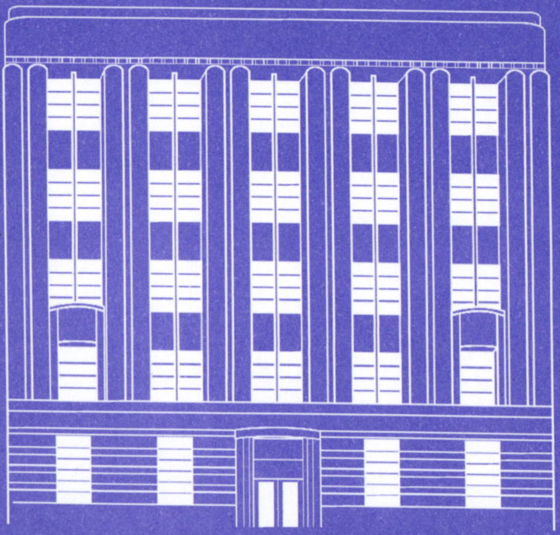

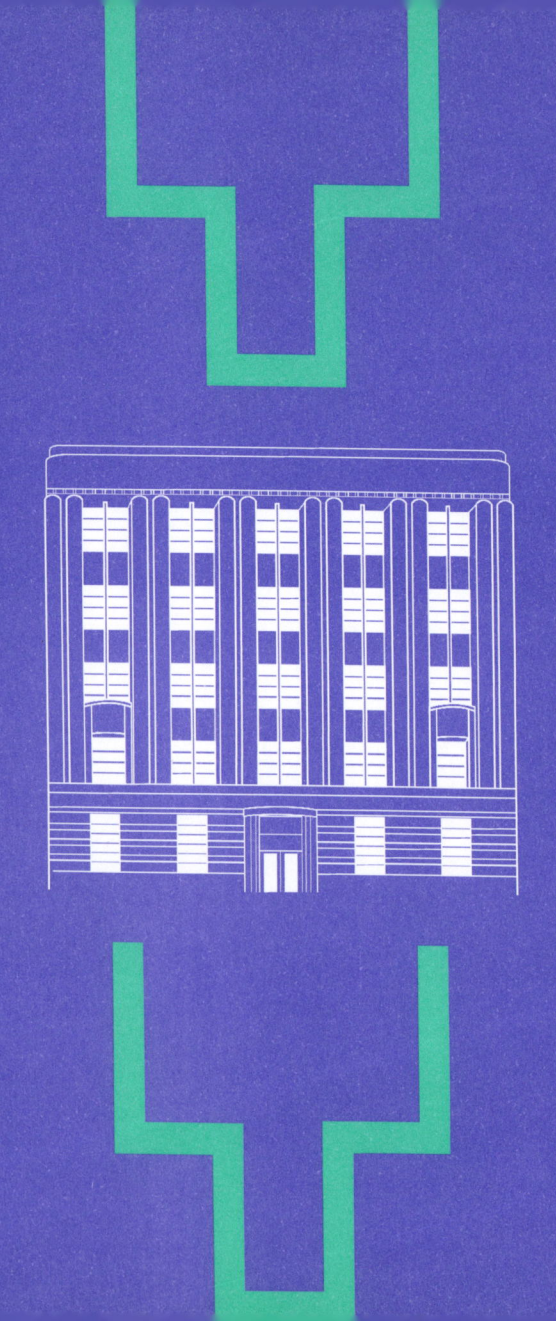

2 99 Macquarie St / 1938 / Budden & Mackey

TRANSPORT HOUSE

Transport House was constructed in order to accommodate the entire Department of Road Transport and Tramways under one roof. Previously its functions had been scattered throughout various CBD locations, and the move reflected similar centralisation activities of various government administrative bodies (such as the Department of Education) to the precinct from the 1850s onwards.

The building is a well preserved example of the Stripped Classical style with Art Deco detailing. The Macquarie Street facade is formed in a classical manner with clearly defined base, colonnade and cornice, all clad in honey coloured sandstone. Rising up four floors, the ten fluted pilasters are grouped in pairs and define the five window bays. Window frames and spandrels are bronze and subtly detailed to emphasise the verticality of the facade. The central entrance is framed in red granite with bronze doors, above which sits a bronze relief of the Greek god Hermes. It is one of the many sculptural details featured on the building designed by artist Rayner Hoff, a WW1 veteran who also designed the sculptures and reliefs for the Hyde Park ANZAC memorial.

Extending across the block, the Phillip Street facade boasts a further three storeys and is designed with more emphasis on the Art Deco style. Flanked by two brick-faced bays, the central recessed facade sits on a simplified base and features seven expressed sandstone fins that are stepped beyond the top level.

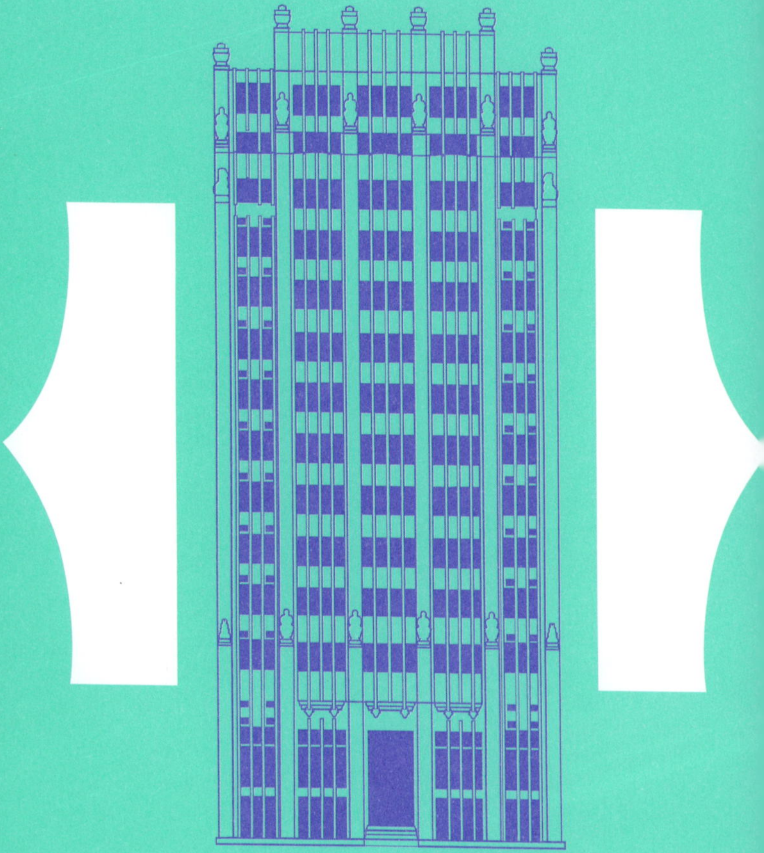

3 135-137 Macquarie St / 1930 / Fowell and McConnel

BMA HOUSE

Founded in England in 1832, the British Medical Association was responsible for the promotion and protection of the medical profession and its activities. In 1879 branches were established in Victoria, NSW and Queensland. By the 1920s the NSW branch, under the secretaryship of Dr Robert Todd, was flourishing and lots 17 and 18 in Macquarie Street had been acquired for the proposed construction of a new headquarters.

Rising to 12 storeys the building was designed in the Skyscraper Gothic manner which was popular in the United States at the time. Early examples such as the Woolworth Building in New York (1913) exhibited elements which would become signatures of the style such as soaring vertical forms and cathedral-like detailing. BMA House possesses many of these attributes including a facade clad in glazed terracotta tiles. Referred to as 'faience', tiled finishes were used extensively in American commercial architecture from the 1890s to the 1930s and made popular in Australia by architects such as Harry Norris in Melbourne (The Nicholas Building, 1926).

One of Sydney's tallest buildings at the time, the facade of BMA House is dominated by three central expressed window bays with ornately tiled spandrels and mullions decorated with rope-like mouldings. Various sculptures adorn the building including winged gargoyles hanging above the ground level, four granite lions on the third and a pair of koalas flanking the eleventh. Where the facade steps back at level 12 six knights can be seen crouching behind their shields which display the Rod of Asclepius (associated with medicine and health care).

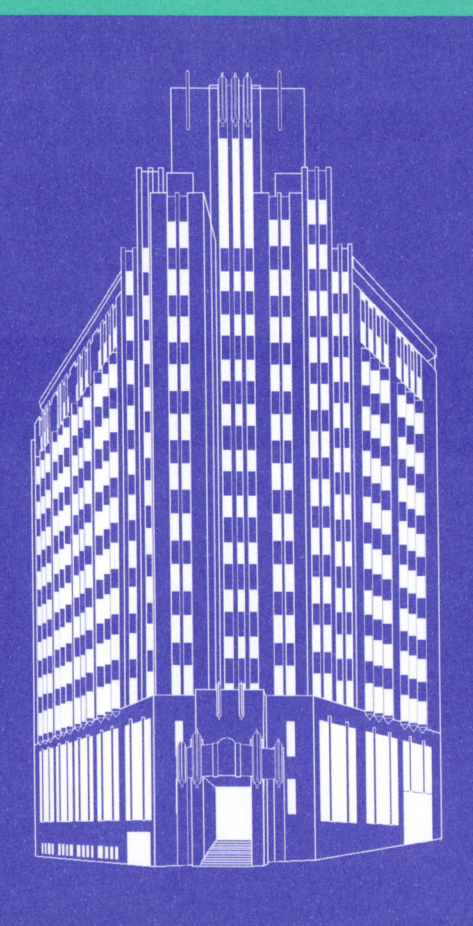

4 60-66 Hunter St / 1936 / Emil Sodersten

CITY MUTUAL LIFE BUILDING

From the 1850s onwards, sparked largely by the discovery of gold, Australia's major cities witnessed enormous economic growth. The increased economic activity and associated risks prompted the establishment of numerous insurance companies throughout the late 19th century. Founded in 1878, the City Mutual Life Assurance Company first erected an office building on the Hunter and Bligh Streets corner site in 1893. As the 1930s dawned, having experienced three decades of prosperity, the company decided to rebuild on the site. A design competition was initiated and Emil Sodersten was announced as the winning architect.

Modelled on contemporary American skyscrapers, the City Mutual Building is composed of a steel frame clad in Wondabyne sandstone (from the NSW Central Coast) above a red granite two-storey base. This contrast in cladding materials also highlights the differing window treatments with large bronze-framed glazing used for the ground and first floors and steel framed casement windows above. Designed as six panel units that follow the expressed vertical serrated form of the facade, they lend a unique repetitive textural quality to the surface. Utilising the corner site in dramatic fashion, the central tower structure rises in multiple planes with tall rectangular windows, continuous expressed mullions and decorative finned elements enhancing the verticality. The black granite entrance is decorated with another fine piece by sculptor Rayner Hoff. The copper bas-relief, known as 'The Flight From Vesuvius', depicts a man protecting his family in Pompeii and is flanked by depictions of Australian flora.

When completed in 1936 a contemporary architectural magazine reported that 'the whole of Sydney is talking about the new City Mutual Building... People passing in the trams lean forward to gaze upon it, while those walking up Hunter Street stop to admire its streamlined symmetry'.

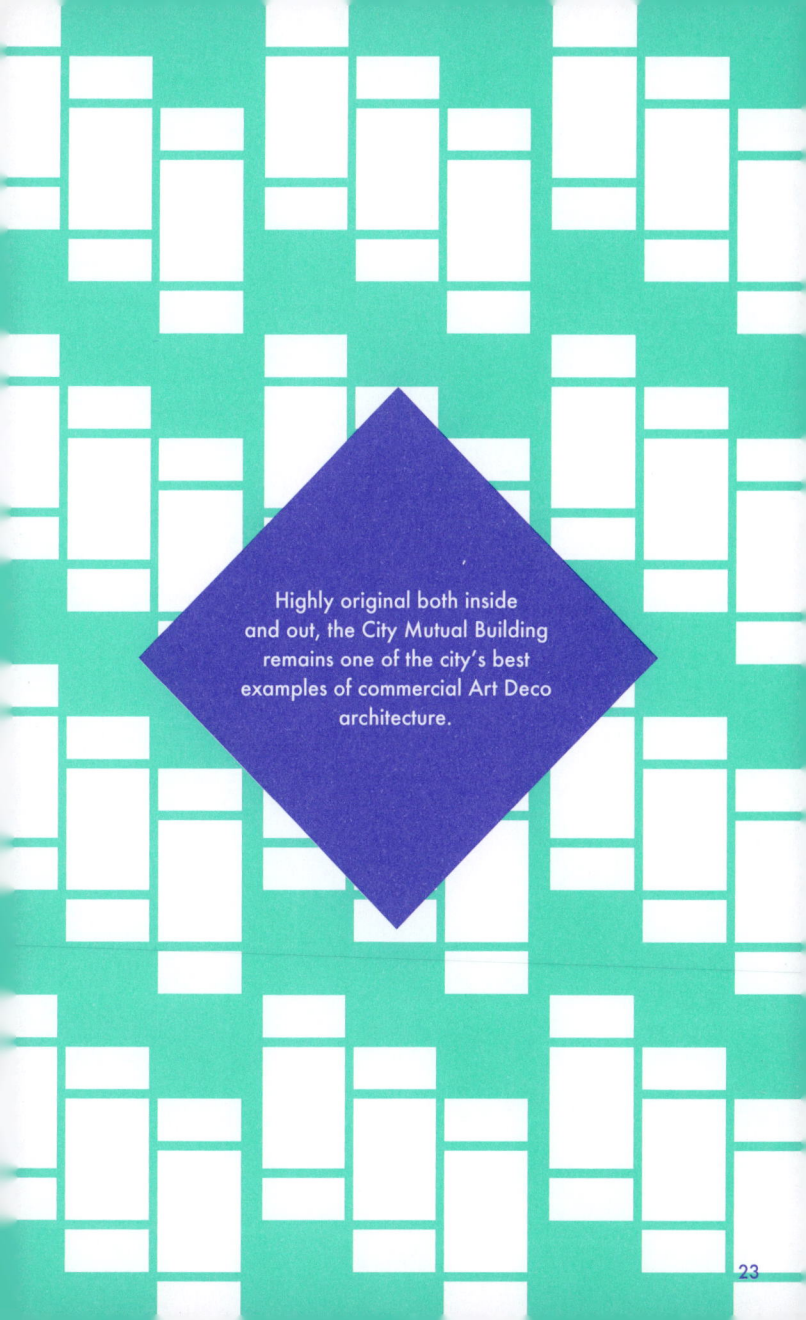

Highly original both inside and out, the City Mutual Building remains one of the city's best examples of commercial Art Deco architecture.

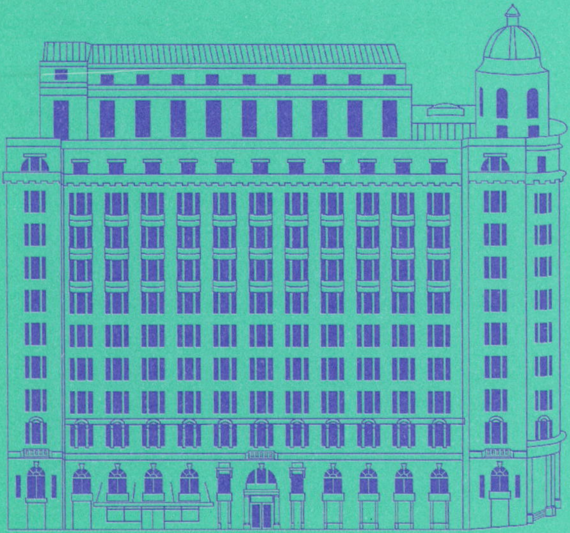

5 64 Pitt St / 1929 / Manson & Pickering

SYDNEY MORNING HERALD BUILDING

The Sydney Herald newspaper was founded in 1831 by former employees of the Sydney Gazette which existed from 1803 to 1842. In 1841 the paper was purchased by John Fairfax who renamed it The Sydney Morning Herald. Fairfax, who had arrived in Sydney from England in 1838 with just £5 in his pocket, went on to establish a business empire that survives to this day as Fairfax Media.

The site at the corner of Pitt, Hunter and O'Connell Streets had been home to the paper since 1856, when Fairfax was joined by his son James in the family business. By 1920 the newspaper had outgrown the premises and a new office building was planned for the site. The new headquarters was constructed in three stages from 1924 to 1929 with the 1856 building being used until stage one was completed. The new design reflected the popular Commercial Palazzo style that emerged from the United States during the early 20th century. Less progressive than contemporary Chicago School architecture, Commercial Palazzo utilised modern internal engineering techniques (steel or concrete frames) but continued with classically derived external forms and decoration.

The sandstone building sits on a two-storey base of smooth-faced rusticated trachyte. Above ground level decoration is generally sparse with curved pediments capping the second floor windows and a series of Doric order pilasters adorning levels six to nine.

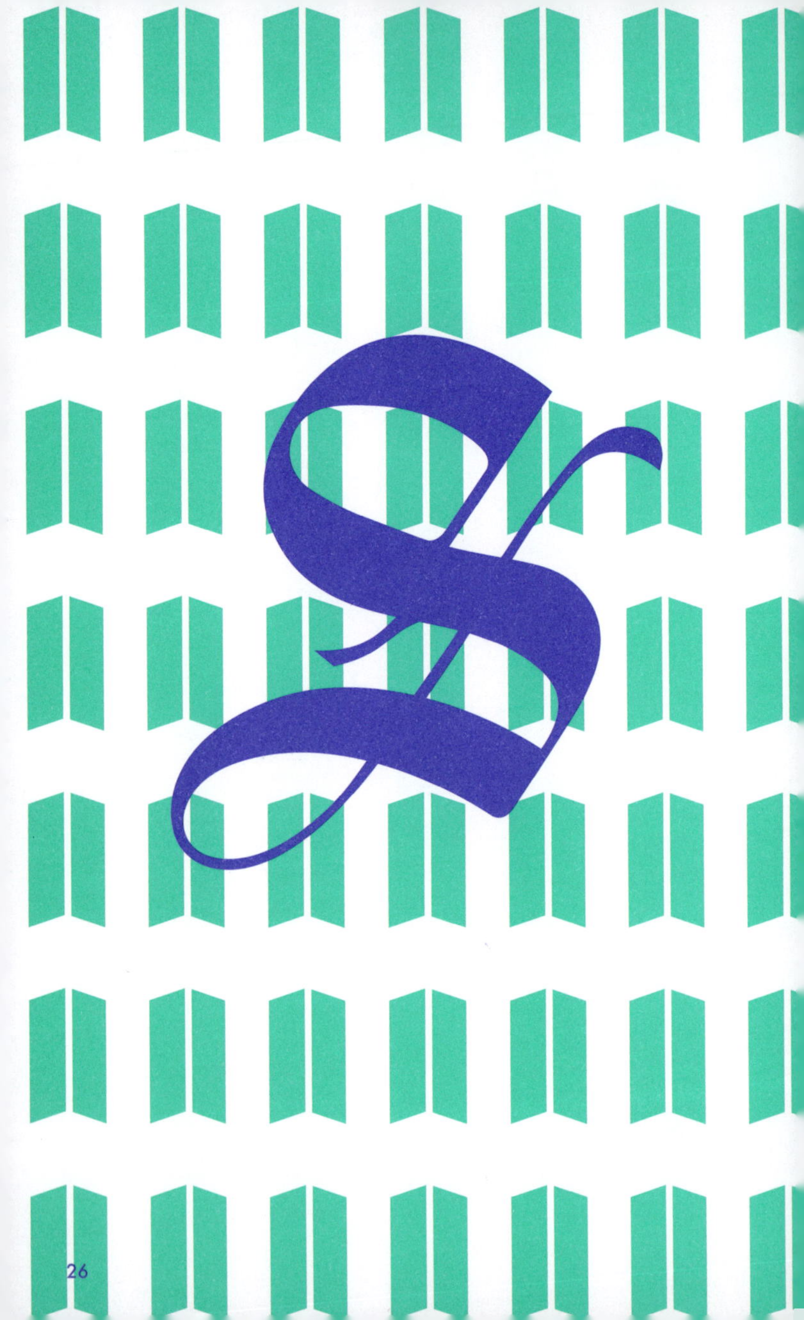

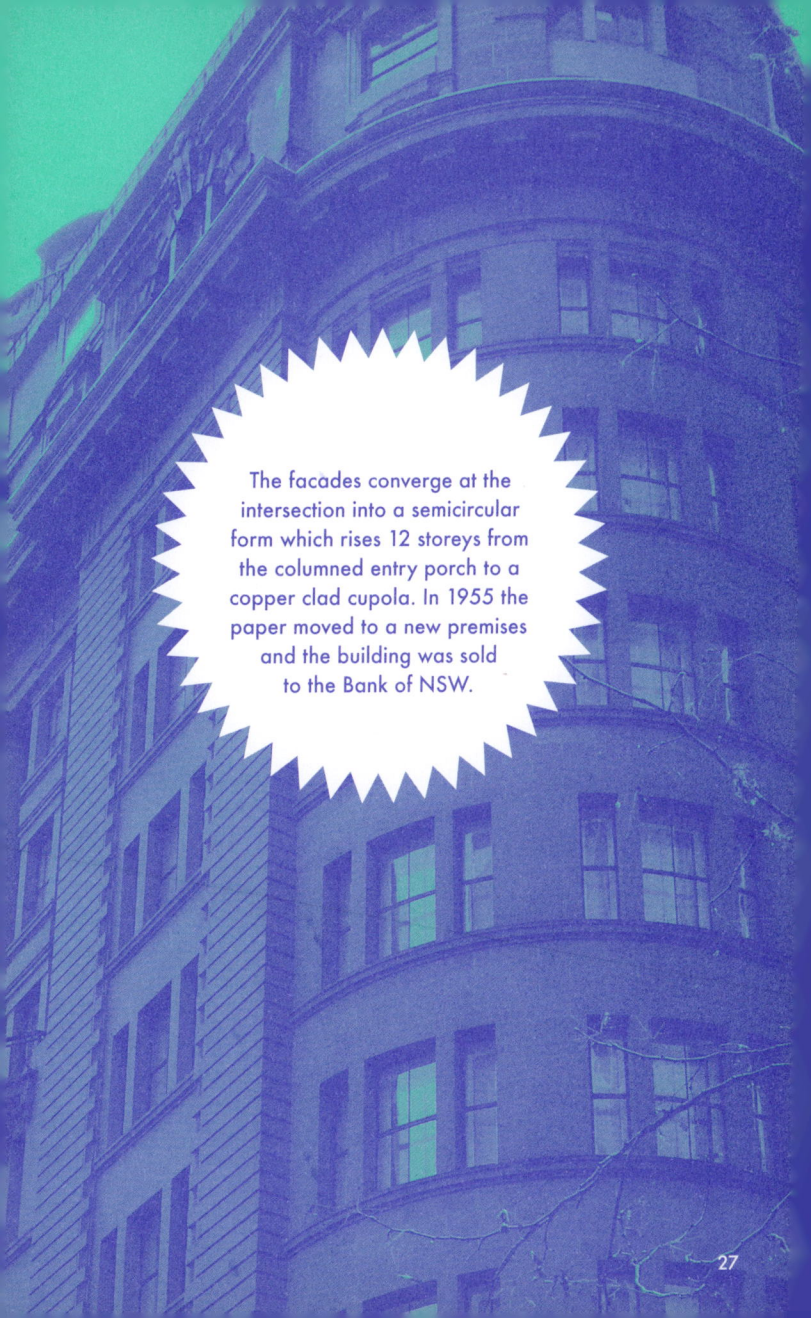

The façades converge at the intersection into a semicircular form which rises 12 storeys from the columned entry porch to a copper clad cupola. In 1955 the paper moved to a new premises and the building was sold to the Bank of NSW.

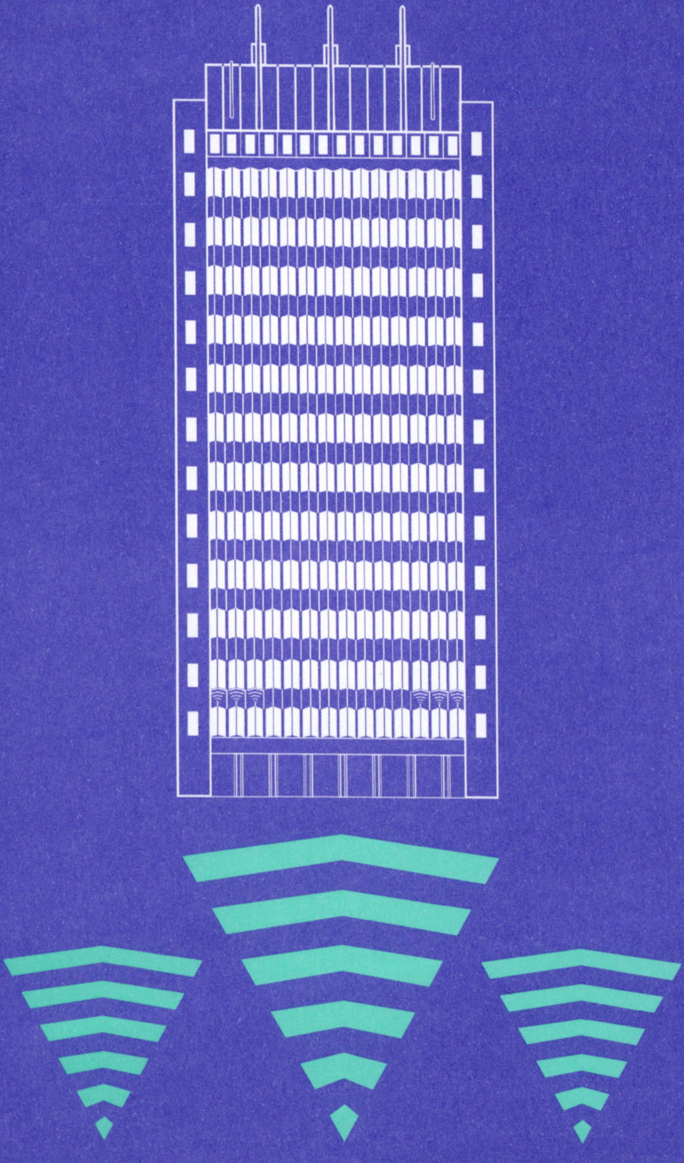

6 80-82 Pitt St / 1939 / Emil Sodersten

BRYANT HOUSE

Three years after the construction of the City Mutual headquarters Emil Sodersten was commissioned by the insurance company to design a building to be used as an investment property.

The architect once again produced a dramatic serrated facade treatment, although this time using brick. The effect is greatly enhanced by the framing of the surface on either side by flat planes, in addition to the richer textural qualities of the brick elements as opposed to the smooth-faced sandstone of the City Mutual Building. Raised above a polished granite plinth the fenestration extends 12 floors to a row of square recessed windows. A trio of vertical fins decorate the upper facade and continue over the roof parapet.

When completed Bryant House attracted a great deal of attention, not only for the exterior but for the lavish use of materials in the interior.

Whilst many of the original fittings have been removed or altered, the entry foyer and lift lobby retain Art Deco details including marble floors, decorative plaster elements and pressed metal ceilings.

✪ OF NOTE

St James Station / 1926 / George McRae

Designed by NSW Government Architect George McRae,
St James station opened in 1926 as part of the new eastern city line.
The Stripped Classical Elizabeth Street entrance (opposite David Jones)
features a stepped sandstone parapet with a decorative cartouche
indicating the 1926 construction date. Inside the entrance, sheltered
by a pressed-metal awning, is an original 1930s neon sign promoting
Chateau Tanunda brandy, a rare surviving example of pre-war
commercial advertising.

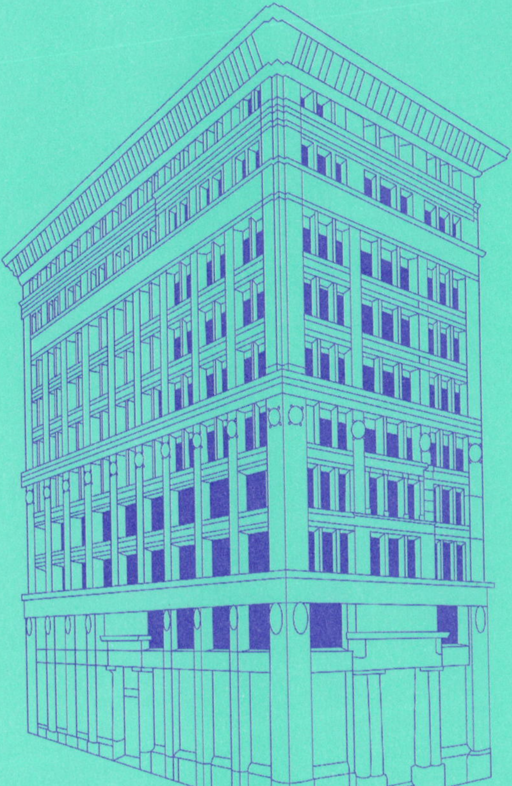

7 108-120 Pitt St / 1916 / John Kirkpatrick

COMMONWEALTH BANK BUILDING

As the first fully steel framed structure in Sydney and the Commonwealth Bank's first national headquarters, this building holds an important place in the architectural and financial history of the city. The Commonwealth Bank of Australia was founded in 1911 as a commercial enterprise by the Labor Government under Prime Minister Andrew Fisher. Opening its first branch in Melbourne in 1912, it expanded via trade through post offices and, by 1913, had branches in all states. Locating its first head office in Sydney's CBD confirmed for many the city's role as Australia's financial capital.

An early example of Commercial Palazzo architecture in Sydney, the Martin Place facade is divided into four distinct sections via the use of differing materials and decorative elements. Smooth-faced trachyte clads the entry level with rusticated pilasters rising to a series of ornate cartouches. The remaining upper sections are clad in sandstone with the second and third sections featuring square pilasters capped with, respectively, shield motifs and Ionic capitals. The top section is punctuated by small recessed windows and is crowned by a broad cornice supported by multiple corbels.

Completed in 1916 the building was subject to two major subsequent additions; the first from 1929-1933 which extended the bank along Pitt Street and was architecturally sympathetic to the original building; the second, undertaken in 1965, extended the Martin Place facade and was designed in a late Stripped Classical manner.

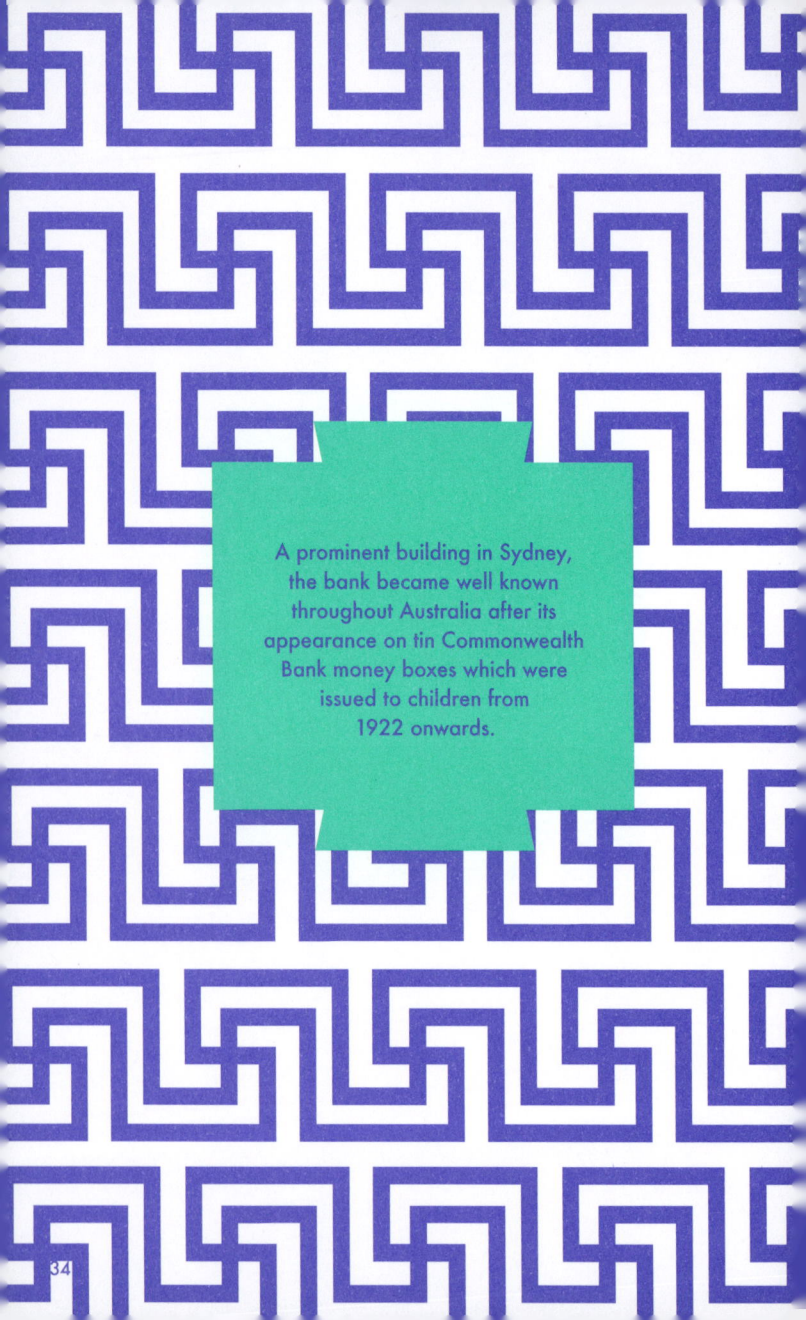

A prominent building in Sydney, the bank became well known throughout Australia after its appearance on tin Commonwealth Bank money boxes which were issued to children from 1922 onwards.

35

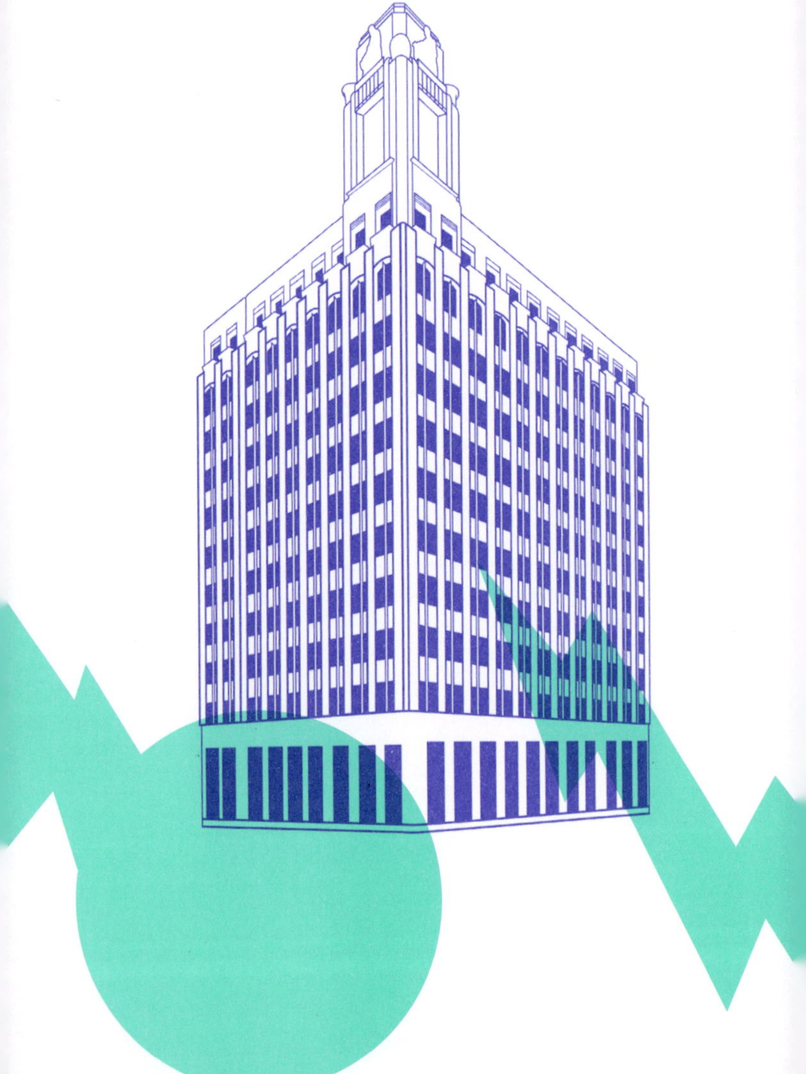

8 42-46 Martin Pl / 1938 / Bate Smart & McCutcheon

MLC BUILDING

By the mid-1930s those businesses that had managed to weather the worst years of the Great Depression were eager to move forward into a more prosperous era. The directors of the Mutual Life and Citizens Assurance Society demonstrated great optimism in the economic future by deciding to construct a new company headquarters on the site they had occupied since the late 1800s.

A design competition was held in 1936 and, from an initial list of 70 entries, the Melbourne firm of Bates, Smart & McCutcheon was chosen for the job. Founded in 1853 by Joseph Reed, it was one of Australia's most distinguished architectural firms and responsible for many of Melbourne's finest Victorian-era buildings, including the State Library and the 1880 Exhibition Buildings.

The Stripped Classical design of the MLC building comprises sandstone-clad facades raised upon a ground floor base of red granite. Sandstone piers, extending unbroken to the ninth floor, divide the fenestration into bays of twin rectangular windows, which are divided by rounded sandstone mullions. The spandrels are enamelled steel panels with horizontal fluted patterning. At the termination of the window bays, above the arched ninth floor windows, are a series of 'hollow and roll' or 'gorge' cornice forms. These are derived from ancient Egyptian architecture and reflect the fashion for using such motifs during the Art Deco period. Further motifs can be found on the corner tower in the form of papyrus shaped columns.

The tower also displays sculpted reliefs of a figure attempting to break a bundle of rods, under which is carved the company motto "Union is Strength".

The Sydney MLC project saw the beginning of a longstanding relationship between the company and Bates Smart & McCutcheon, with the firm being commissioned for numerous MLC office buildings around Australia throughout the 1950s.

✪ OF NOTE

State Savings Bank of New South Wales
48-50 Martin Place / 1928 / H E Ross & Rowe

Next to the MLC Building (across Castlereagh Street) sits the former headquarters of the State Savings Bank. Constructed in an imposing Beaux Arts style the building was taken over by the Commonwealth Bank in 1931 and subsequently, along with the bank's Pitt Street headquarters, became the subject for a tin money box design. The red granite and pink terracotta tiled exterior is matched by an elaborate interior that visitors are encouraged to explore.

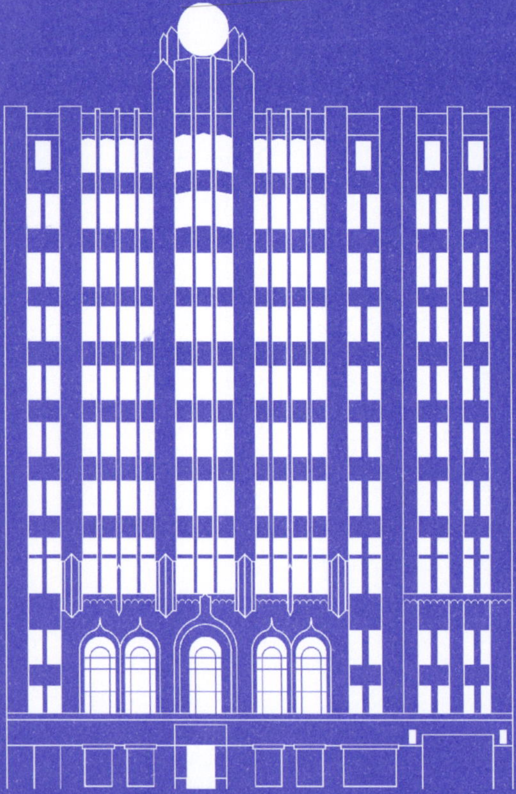

9 60-70 Elizabeth St / 1929 / J Kethel

SUN BUILDING

The first in Sydney to be designed in the Skyscraper Gothic style, the former Sun building was also the last of the major newspaper-based offices to be constructed in the city. Sir Hugh Robert Denison came from a wealthy family whose fortune had been made in the tobacco industry. He founded Sun Newspapers Ltd in 1910 and rapidly expanded the business via the acquisition of various rival papers. The company purchased the lot between Elizabeth and Phillip Streets in 1921 in anticipation of the city council's extension plans for Martin Place, which would see the demolition of their existing offices.

The new headquarters, designed by Joseph Alexander Kethel, was officially opened on 15 October 1929 by the Governor of NSW, Sir Dudley de Chair. Kethel had previously designed numerous buildings for Sun Newspapers Ltd including a four-storey office for the Newcastle Sun, a regional paper acquired in 1918.

The Sun building represents a relatively restrained example of Skyscraper Gothic and includes idiosyncratic detailing such as the Tuscan column mullions dividing the first floor arch windows, a feature not usually associated with the style. Above a ground floor base of Uralla granite, the facade is clad in beige panels of Benedict stone (manufactured by the U.S based Benedict Stone Company by pouring a mix of stone dust and cement into moulds). Above the five ogee arch windows decorative mouldings launch piers and mullions upwards, terminating in a series of Gothic pinnacles. The roof is crowned with a sphere atop a small tower which, when the building was first opened, glistened with gold paint.

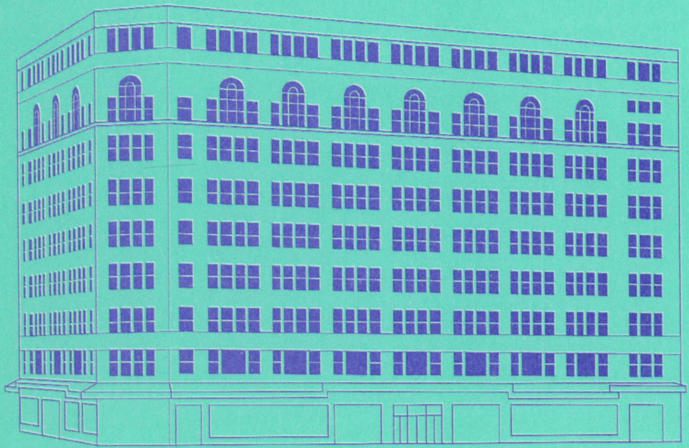

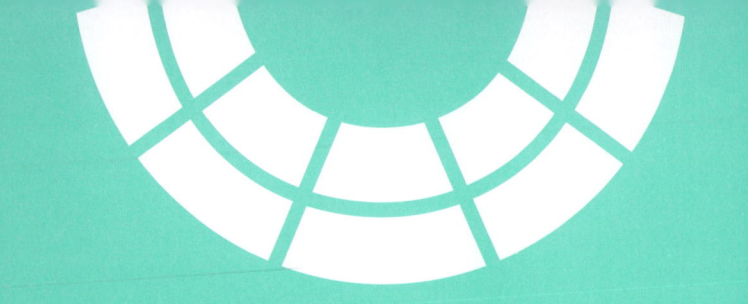

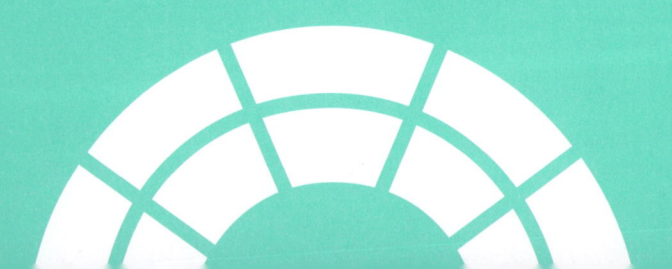

10 Cnr Castlereagh & Market Sts / 1927 & 1938 /
Budden & Mackellar & Mackeller & Partridge

DAVID JONES BUILDINGS

Welsh merchant David Jones moved to Australia in 1835, opening his first store in 1838 on the corner of George and Barrack Streets with the intention of selling "the best and most exclusive goods". By the 1920s the now public company was being run by his grandson Charles Lloyd Jones who announced plans to construct a new store on a recently purchased block of land on Elizabeth Street.

Architectural firm Budden & Mackellar produced an elegant Stripped Classical building befitting the prestige of the client. Clad in sandstone, the facades express a lightness of form due to the steel frame structure that allowed for large rectangular windows divided by slim mullions. The building is divided into distinct sections, the first floor being differentiated by rusticated stone and the top by the use of multi-paned arched windows. The original copper-clad awning remains in place above street level and features decorative urns.

Sited diagonally opposite the 1927 building is the third David Jones store to be constructed in the city. Built to celebrate the company's 100th anniversary it was designed by the firm Mackeller & Partridge in the contemporary Streamline Moderne style. Contrasting with the classic angularity of the store opposite, the 1938 sandstone facade curves around the corner, emphasising the dynamic horizontality of the glazing bands.

External decoration is kept to a minimum with a ribbed awning and aluminium and glass grid panels above the street entrances. Originally six floors, four floors in the same style were added in 1951.

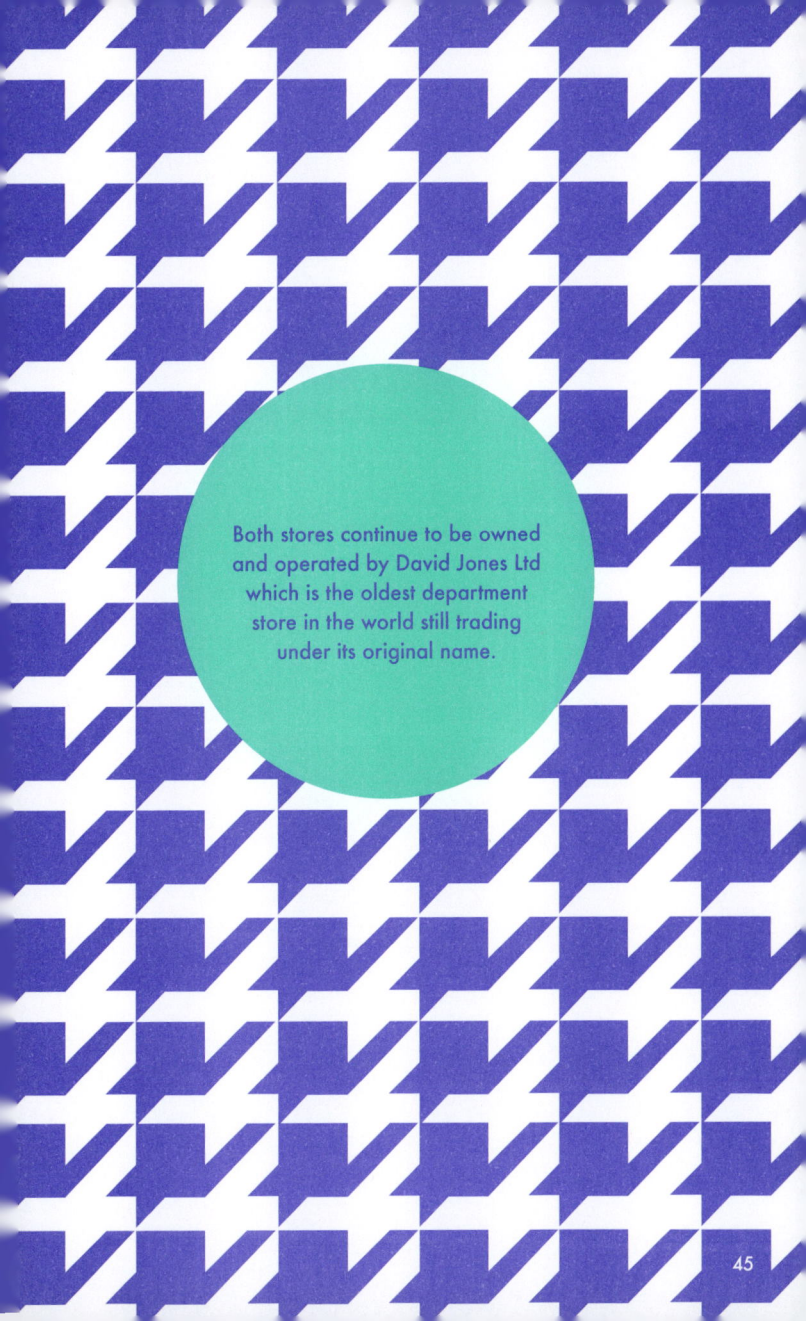

Both stores continue to be owned and operated by David Jones Ltd which is the oldest department store in the world still trading under its original name.

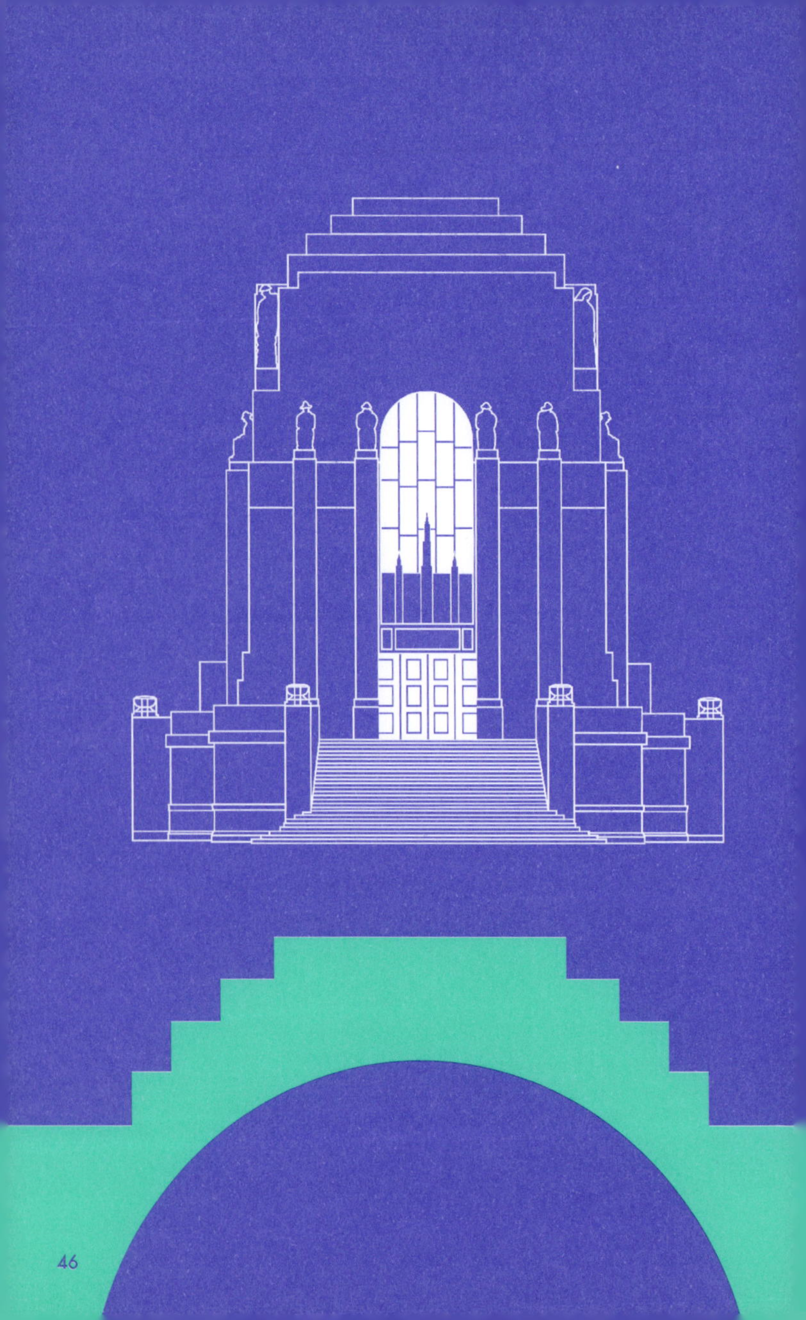

11 Hyde Park / 1934 / Charles Bruce Dellit

HYDE PARK ANZAC MEMORIAL

It is a telling indication of the shock and grief felt following the bloody Anzac campaign on Gallipoli that fund raising for a memorial began on the first anniversary of the event (25 April 1916) while the war in Europe was still raging. In 1929 an official design competition was announced and local architect Charles Bruce Dellit produced the winning entry. Dellit had only recently established his private practice and the memorial would be the first of many projects that exhibited his pioneering Art Deco style throughout the 1930s.

Dominating the southern end of Hyde Park the memorial is constructed of concrete clad in pink granite panels. Square in form, the main block features square pilasters on each facade flanking large arched stained glass windows. The structure is crowned with a stepped, ziggurat-style roof.

Adorning the building both inside and out are numerous works by sculptor Raynor Hoff. Stone figures representing military personnel are perched atop the pilasters and roof corners whilst carved relief panels form a band around the structure. Above the east and west doors are ten-metre bronze friezes which depict the various activities and actions of the Australian Imperial Forces.

The interior of the memorial, however, holds the most dramatic of Hoff's pieces. Entering the memorial via ground level brings visitors into the marble-lined vestibule which in turn, leads to the Hall of Memory. Standing in the centre of the hall is 'Sacrifice', a bronze sculpture of a naked fallen soldier lying on a shield supported by three caryatids representing his mother, sister and wife. The naked figure was considered shocking at the time of its unveiling and precluded the installation of two further nudes intended for the exterior.

Opened on 24 November 1934 by Prince Henry, Duke of Gloucester, the memorial is considered to be Charles Bruce Dellit's finest Art Deco work.

50

12 143-147 Liverpool St / 1909-1928 / McCredie & Anderson, H E Ross & Rowe

FOYS BUILDING

The Mark Foys Emporium building as it stands today is the result of major inter-war additions made to the original two-storey structure of 1909.

Irish immigrant Mark Foy ran a series of successful drapery stores in Melbourne during the 1870s and 80s, handing the business over to his two sons in 1882. In 1885, following a move to Sydney, Francis and Mark Foy Jr opened a store on Oxford Street. The business flourished and in 1909 the brothers constructed one of the grandest department stores the city had seen. Partly inspired by the pioneering Bon Marche department store in Paris (1852), the initial two-storey design was an interesting mix of early 20th century Chicagoesque and late 19th century Second Empire architectural styles. The 1928 extensions, which saw the construction of an additional four storeys, were designed in a similar manner.

Skirted by a large awning decorated with pressed metal soffits, the facades are clad with white glazed bricks, dramatically setting off the ornate yellow faience elements. Panels on the first level advertise goods available in the store while those on the second are adorned with floral motifs. Rising above a simple cornice with corbels, the 1928 facade features square pilasters with Corinthian capitals dividing wide window bays. The upper level, adorned with green Solomonic column mullions, is topped on the Liverpool Street elevation by ornate gabled parapets flanked by two prominent mansard roofed towers.

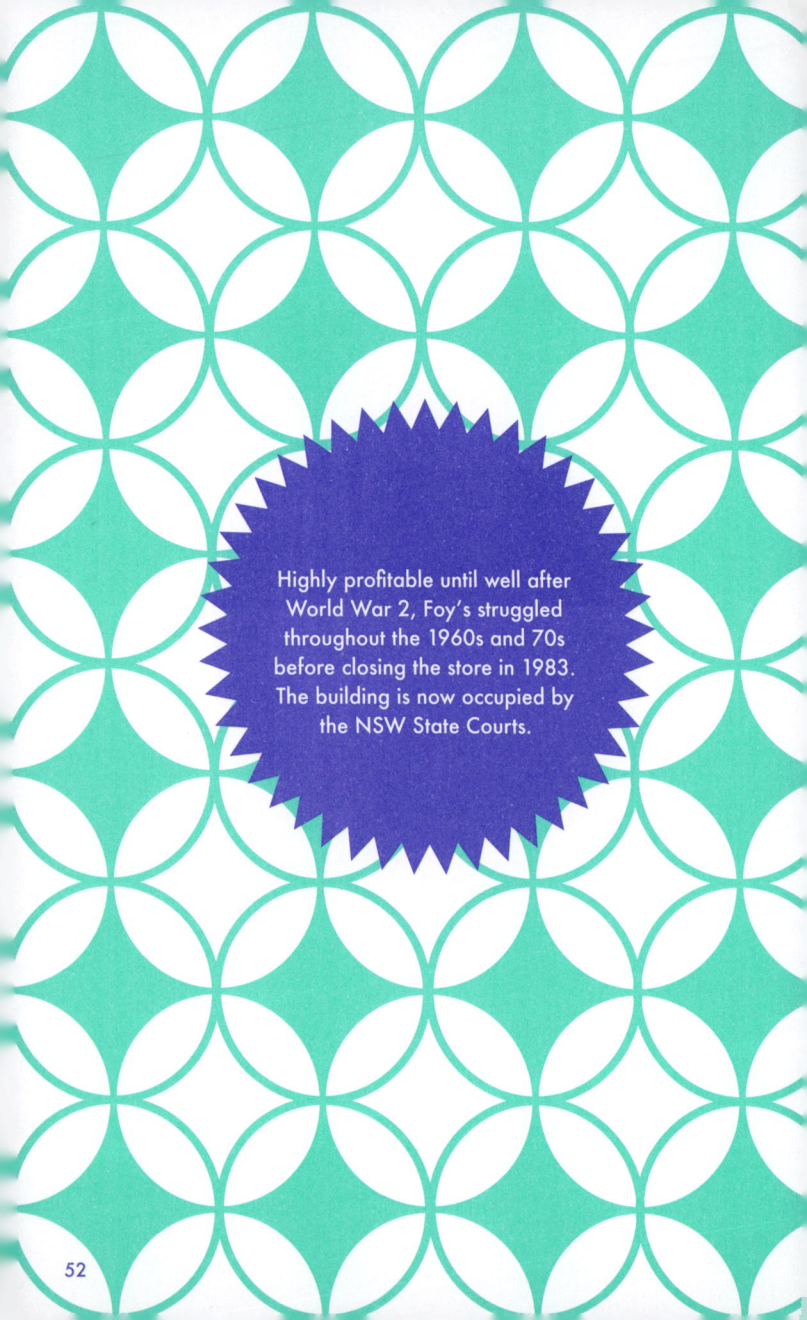

Highly profitable until well after World War 2, Foy's struggled throughout the 1960s and 70s before closing the store in 1983. The building is now occupied by the NSW State Courts.

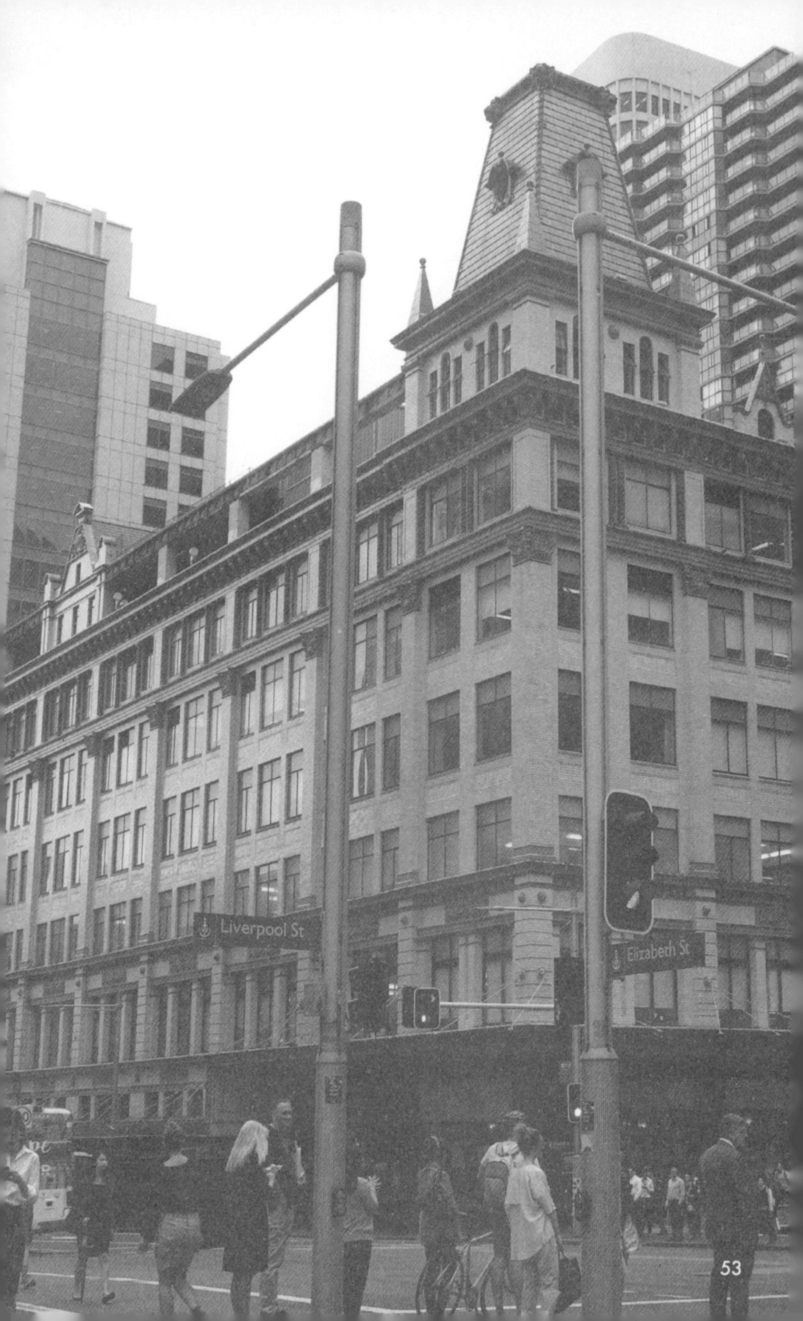
Liverpool St
Elizabeth St

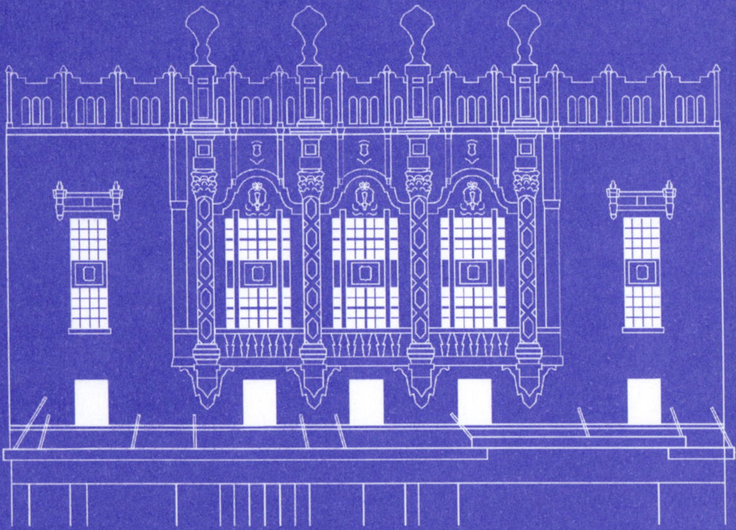

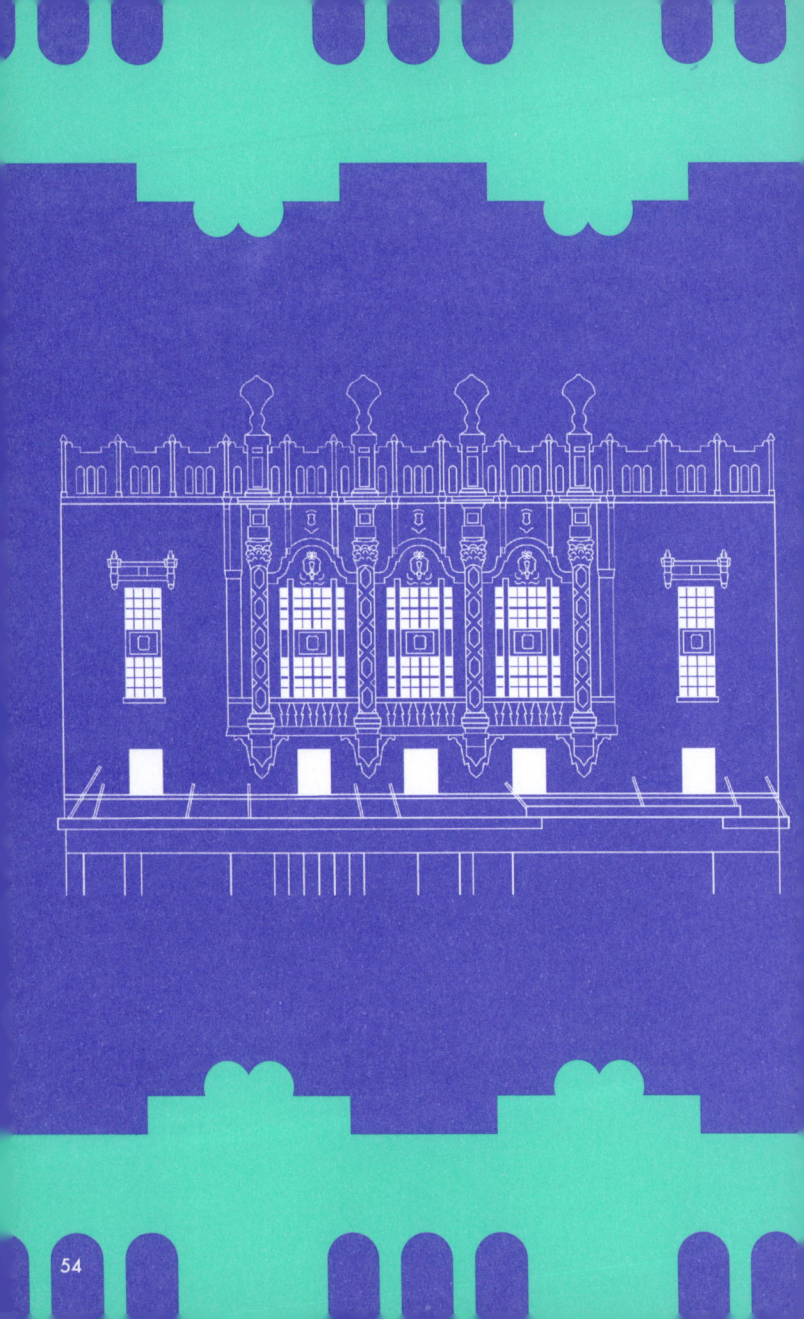

13 600 George St / 1930 / Eric Heath

PLAZA THEATRE

Throughout the 1920s and 30s cinemas, or picture palaces as they were known in the UK and Australia, were often designed in a style that represented the escapist glamour displayed on the screens within. The 2000 seat Plaza Theatre, with its Spanish Baroque detailing, was certainly no exception.

Built for the Hoyts Group the theatre is constructed of brick with a textured render finish and precast concrete decoration. The George Street facade is chamfered on both sides and dominated by a highly ornate central arrangement of pilasters and arched windows.
The four pilasters are decorated with geometric relief patterns and topped by Corinthian capitals. Three bays of multi-paned windows are divided by ornate spandrels and are set back from balustraded balconettes. The pilasters rise to individual cornices which further extend to corresponding spiral urns sitting atop the roof parapet.

The years following the end of World War 2 saw a decline in cinema attendance, accelerated by the introduction of television to Australian cities in 1956. Although the Plaza ceased to function as a cinema in 1977, it escaped the terminal fate of many other city theatres through the utilisation of the venue for various entertainment purposes over the years. Initially converted to a skating rink, the auditorium has also been used as a live concert venue and restaurant. A McDonald's restaurant has occupied the foyer since 1977, the only part of the theatre that still retains its original interior elements including roof beams and decorative Spanish motifs.

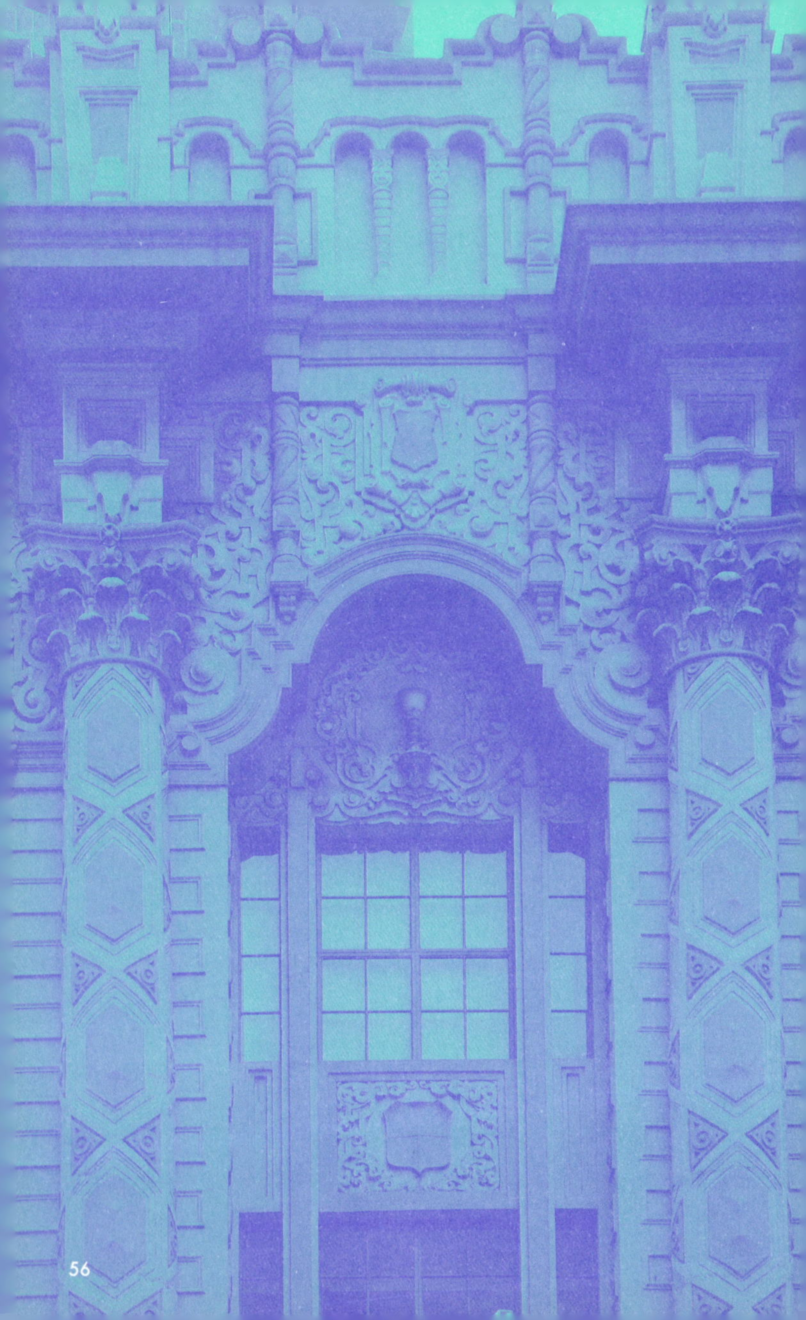

✪ OF NOTE

Bebarfalds / 1929 / Kent & Massie

Furniture and homewares retailer Bebarfalds occupied the prestigious site opposite Sydney Town Hall (cnr George and Park Streets) from 1894. The building that exists today was constructed in 1929, initially to eight levels. The Stripped Classical design sits on a rusticated base and features a simple square fenestration treatment with decorative spandrel panels on the seventh floor. The second floor was originally used for display rooms including an entire fully furnished, six room Spanish Bungalow style home. Two additional floors were added in 1967, shortly before a takeover by Ajax Insurance Ltd.

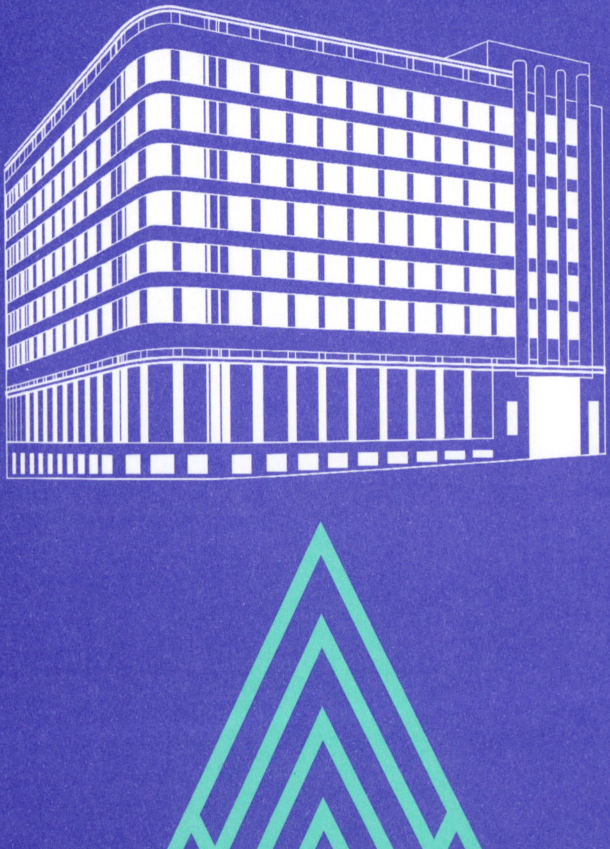

14 339-341 Pitt St / 1939 / Budden & Mackey

METROPOLITAN WATER, SEWERAGE & DRAINAGE BOARD BUILDING

With the 1939 Metropolitan Water Sewerage & Drainage Board building, architects Budden & Mackey not only provided a modern headquarters for the organisation but gave Sydney what is now considered one of the city's finest and most exquisitely detailed Art Deco structures.

The Government entity now known as Sydney Water was formed in 1888, initially occupying offices at Circular Quay. In 1890 the department moved to Pitt Street where it remained throughout various office renovations and expansions until a 2009 move to Parramatta. The 1939 building dramatically demonstrates the stylistic development of the Art Deco architectural movement from the vertical angularity of the 1920s to the horizontal streamlined forms of the late 1930s. Facade elements are clearly articulated by the use of contrasting materials beginning with a ground-level base of red granite cladding framing a colonnade of black granite piers. Wide horizontal bronze banding and yellow faience mullions frame the upper level bronze windows, rounding the corner in a smooth transition.

The main entrance is marked by four vertical faience clad fins which extend up the height of the facade, forming three bays of smaller bronze windows. Three bas relief panels, sculpted by Stanley Hammond, sit above the entrance and depict mankind's dependence upon water. After the departure of Sydney Water the interior was refurbished for use as a luxury hotel, although many of the original materials and elements have been retained.

GOWINGS

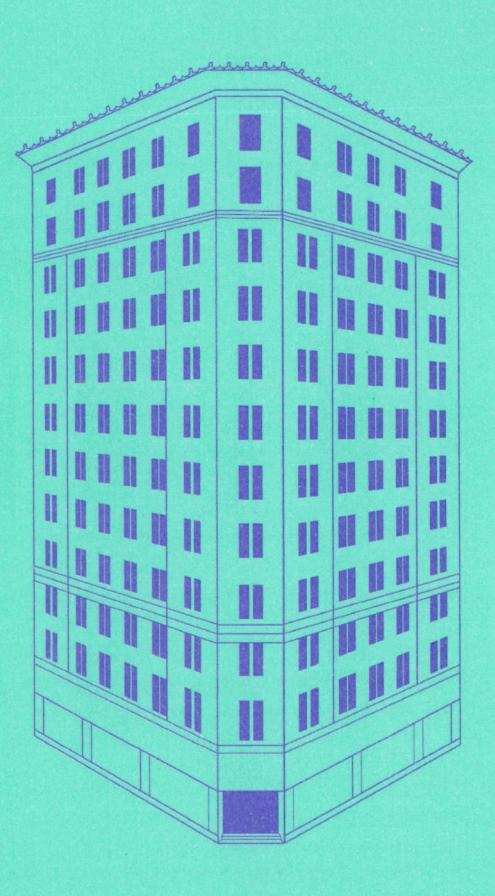

15 452 George St / 1929 / C.H MacKeller

GOWINGS BUILDING

On 29 January 2006, after years of declining sales, the Gowings store on George Street closed its doors for the last time. Established in 1868 by John Gowing and his brother Preston, the menswear retailer was a deeply entrenched Sydney institution with stores throughout the city and suburbs. One of the company's post-war advertising slogans, "Gone to Gowings", had even made its way into the local vernacular as meaning a person or thing was missing or irretrievably lost.

Designed in the Commercial Palazzo style, the building on the corner of George and Market Streets was purpose-built for Gowings, becoming their flagship CBD store. Clad in sandstone, the 12 storey structure presents two street facades flanking a chamfered corner. The first and second floors are rusticated with squared pilasters extending to an entablature and cornice. The restrained mid-section is composed of clearly articulated sandstone blocks punctuated by sash windows and separated from the upper two levels by a simple cornice form. Decorative details of the lower levels are repeated at the top section with the addition of corbelled window ledges and ornate pilaster capitals.

Since the departure of Gowings the building's interior has been extensively refurbished and is now home to a major UK based fashion retailer and luxury hotel. The Gowings signage adorning the facades has also been restored and now advertises an upscale bar and grill restaurant in the building.

✪ OF NOTE

State Theatre / 1929 / Henry E. White

Next door to Gowings is the spectacular State Theatre. Completed just before the Great Depression, the building is a flamboyant showcase of theatrical architectural and decorative styles.

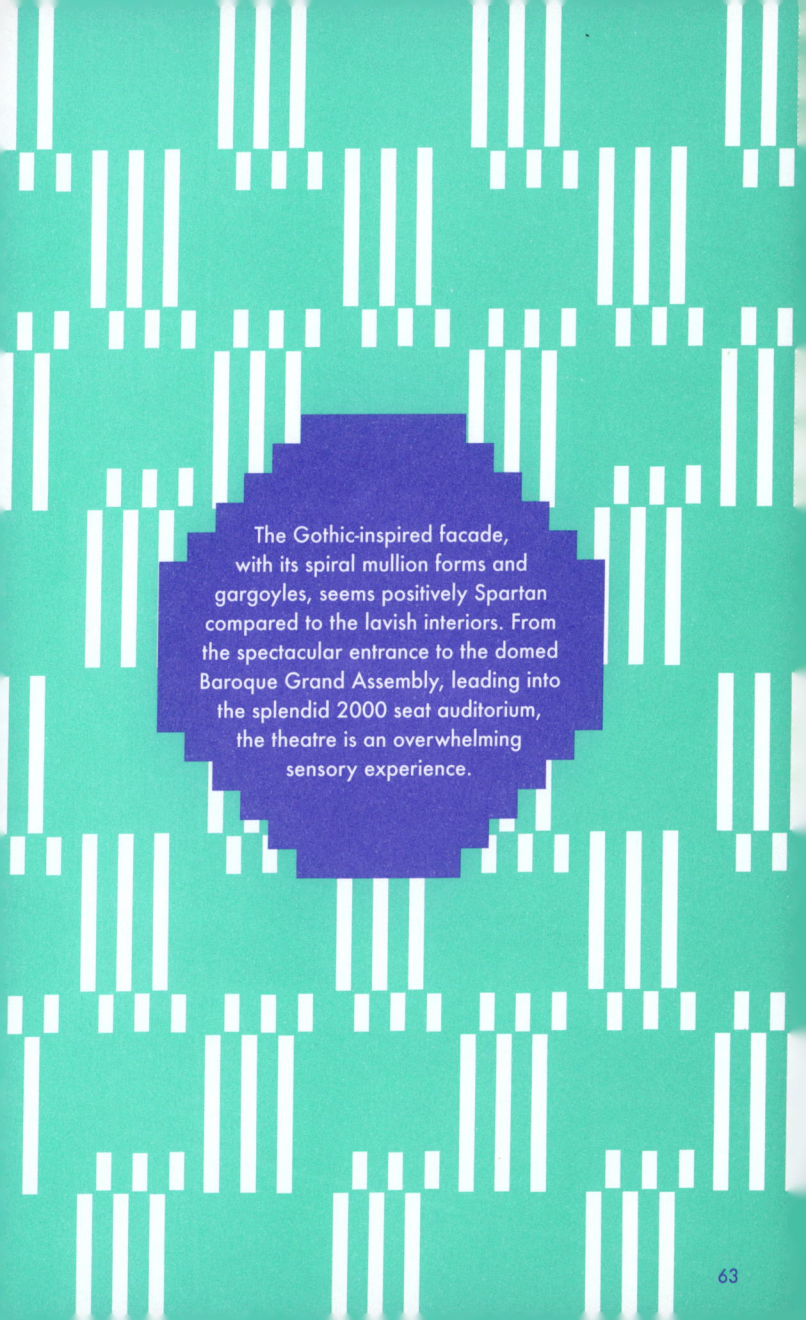

The Gothic-inspired facade, with its spiral mullion forms and gargoyles, seems positively Spartan compared to the lavish interiors. From the spectacular entrance to the domed Baroque Grand Assembly, leading into the splendid 2000 seat auditorium, the theatre is an overwhelming sensory experience.

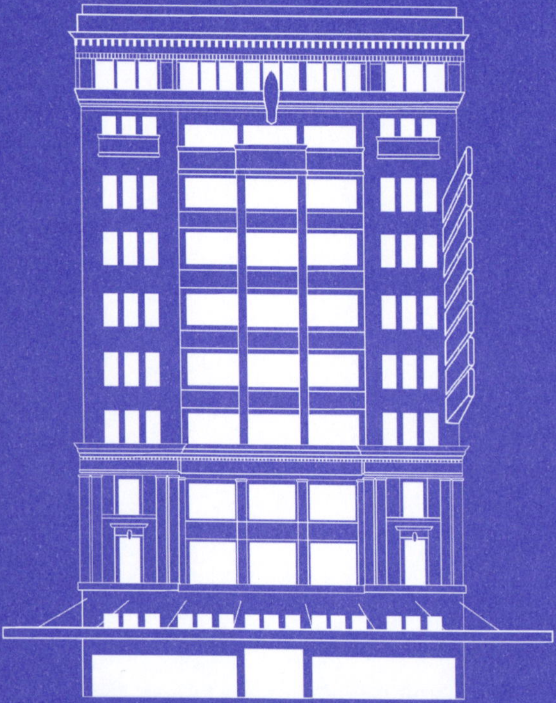

16 428 George St / 1932 / F.H.B Wilton

DYMOCKS BUILDING

Beginning in 1879 with a small store on Market Street, by the 1890s Dymocks Booksellers claimed to be "the largest book shop in the world, holding upwards of one million books". The founder, William Dymock, died in 1900 aged just 39 and the business was subsequently run by his sister, Marjory, and her husband John Forsyth. At the time the bookstore was operating out of a leased shop that was part of the Royal Hotel building on George Street, an arrangement that continued into the 1920s. By 1922 the continuing success of the business enabled the Forsyth family to purchase the Royal Hotel site with the intention of constructing a flagship bookstore and shopping arcade.

Construction commenced in 1926 but wasn't completed until 1932 due to financial difficulties caused by the Great Depression. The 11 storey building, with its clearly divided facade sections, is an interesting example of the Commercial Palazzo style. Clad in unusual grey 'granite' terracotta, the lower levels form a classic base of vertical forms including square Doric pilasters terminating at a simple entablature with dentilled cornice. The middle section is composed of three distinct bays, the central bay being clad in a Chicagoesque curtain wall of bronze spandrels and mullions. The flanking bays are punctuated with simple unadorned rectangular windows with the exception of corbelled balconies on the tenth floor. A decorative cartouche sits atop the central facade, above which sits the top level crowned by an elaborate entablature.

'The Block', as the building is also known, refers to the shopping arcade above the Dymocks store, occupied by various small businesses over the years. Accessed via the central street entrance, the interiors are largely original and include terrazzo floors, silky oak shopfronts and leadlight elements.

DYMOCKS

THE BLOCK

SHOP PROMENADES

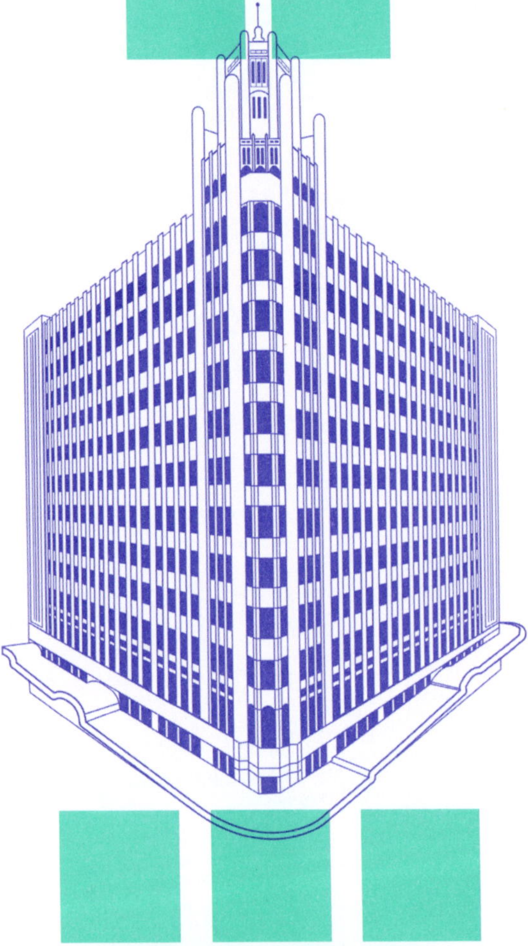

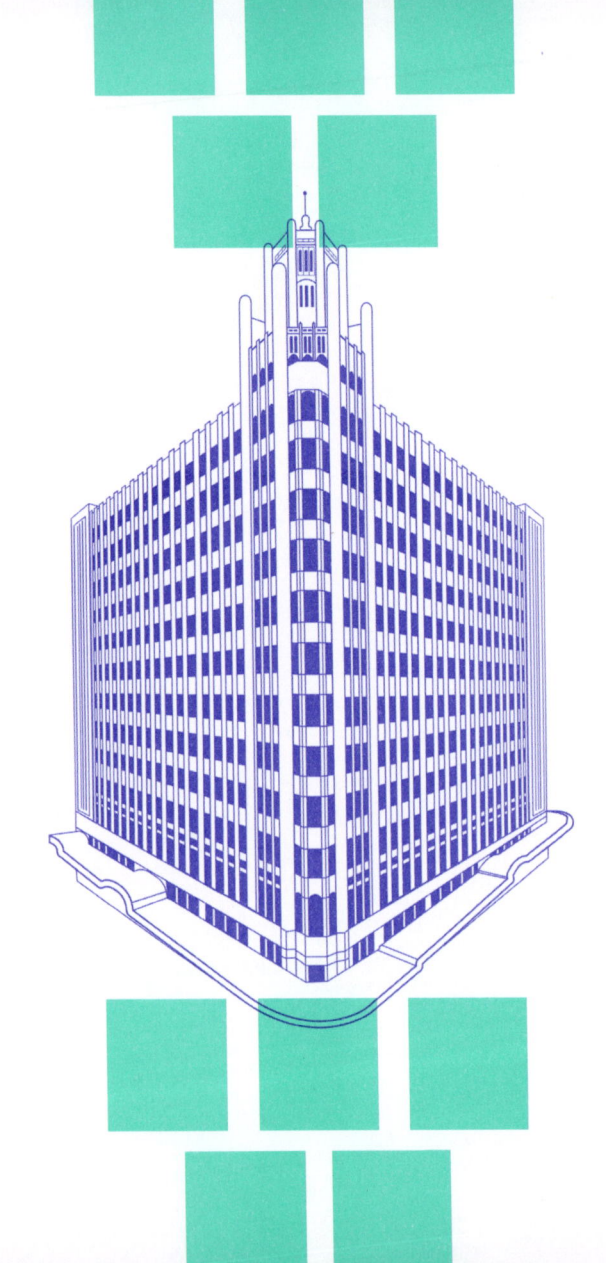

17 77 York St / 1930 / Morrow & Gordon

GRACE BUILDING

The Grace brothers, Albert Edward and Joseph Neal, kicked off their retail enterprise in the 1880s by selling goods door to door throughout Sydney. By the 1920s the firm now known as Grace Bros Ltd was firmly entrenched as one of the city's major retailers and the brothers were looking to construct a new headquarters. Reasoning that the imminent opening of the Sydney Harbour Bridge would direct increasing pedestrian traffic along York and Clarence Streets, a site was purchased in the area in 1926.

Architects Morrow and Gordon were commissioned to design the building, producing a spectacular Skyscraper Gothic structure heavily influenced by the Tribune Tower in Chicago (1925). Clad in cream faience tiles, the soaring verticality of the facades is emphasised by the expressed mullion forms used to divide the fenestration. First floor windows are topped by Gothic arched tracery spandrels highlighted with green panels. The corner features four main pilasters rising beyond the 12th floor to form a buttressed tower.

Opened by Lord Mayor Alderman ES Marks on 3 July, 1930 the building drew immediate praise for its dramatic appearance and modern amenities including the light-filled, well-ventilated offices and high-speed lifts. Utilising the first two levels as a department store, the remaining floors were to be leased out as office space. This proved difficult, however, due to the economic effects of the Great Depression and failure of increased traffic to the area to materialise as previously envisioned.

In 1942 the Australian Government requisitioned the building for use by various Commonwealth Departments, retaining it until well after 1945. After compensating Grace Bros Ltd for the loss of the building in 1953, various government departments worked out of the premises until it was sold to a private hotel group in 1995.

✪ OF NOTE

Asbestos House / 1929 / Robertson & Marks

Sited on the corner of York and Barrack Streets is the former headquarters of building materials firm James Hardie. Grey granite tiles clad the first two levels with the remaining upper floors finished in rendered masonry. The facades are given a strong sense of verticality with continuous mullion forms intersecting pale green spandrels. The Stripped Classical form displays subtle Egyptian inspired Art Deco motifs on the front entrance and roof cornice.

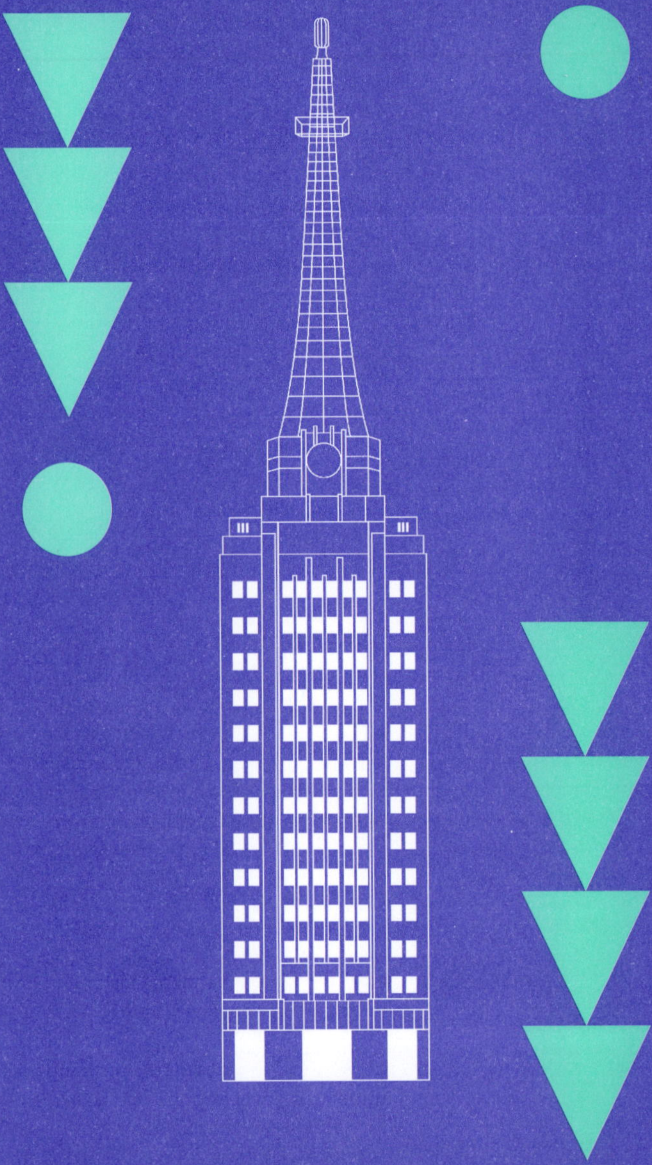

18 45 York St / 1939 / Marks & McCredie, Morrow & Gordon

AWA TOWER

For much of the 20th century Amalgamated Wireless (Australasia) Ltd operated as Australia's largest electronics manufacturer and broadcaster. The company was directly involved in many early communication milestones including receiving the first radio broadcast from the UK to Australia (1918) and transmitting the first newsreel pictures from Sydney to London (1930).

Constructed in 1939 as a new headquarters, AWA Tower clearly communicated the Art Deco movement's integration of architecture and technology. Clad in brick, the facade presents a soaring skyscraper aesthetic with a central six window bay rising beyond narrower flanking bays. The facade steps back to form the base for the communications tower which, at 46 metres on top of the main structure's 55-metres, made AWA Tower the tallest building in Sydney until the 1960s. The tower itself was partly modelled on the Funkturm Berlin (Berlin Radio Tower), constructed in 1926 for the Third Great German Radio Exhibition.

Decoration is minimal with the AWA logo sitting below the tower and a mosaic tiled sculpture of the winged horse 'Pegasus' on the parapet. The entrance level is faced with trachyte which, in its geometric shapes, reflects the termination form of the upper floors. The glass awning with decorative waterfall motifs is a later addition. The entry foyer and lift lobby remain in original decorative form, faced with Wombeyan marble with streamlined details.

AWA didn't survive into the 21st century. It was absorbed into the Jupiter Group which currently owns the building.

75

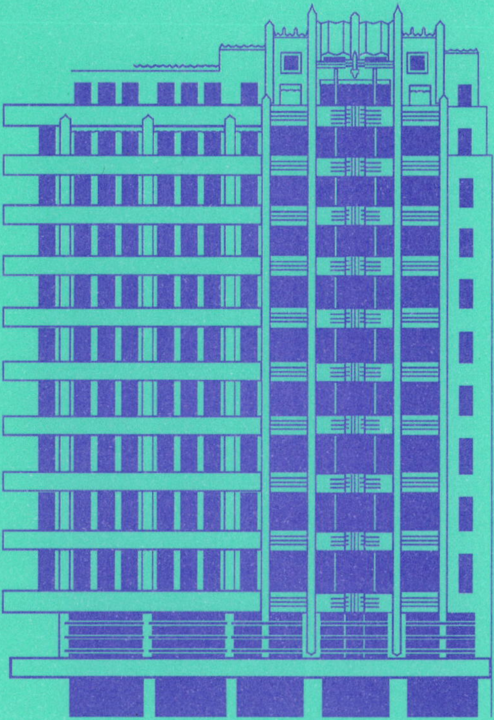

19 19-31 York St / 1935 / Budden & Mackey

RAILWAY HOUSE

Sydney's first suburban train line opened on 26 September 1855, linking the city to Parramatta via four stations. The network rapidly expanded and by 1926 was fully electrified. With the opening of Sydney Harbour Bridge in 1932 the existing North Shore Line was linked to the CBD by the newly constructed Wynyard and Town Hall underground stations. Wynyard station was subsequently chosen as the site for the New South Wales State Railways administrative headquarters, with construction beginning in 1934.

Originally conceived as a dominant central tower flanked by horizontal wings, the final asymmetrical design was well received. It possesses a modern aesthetic with subtle yet dynamic Art Deco detailing. Unbroken horizontal spandrel bands run across the main block, dividing the bronze framed windows into Modernist strips. The tower section rises in three bays created by four vertical fins, terminating in a stepped Deco skyscraper manner at the top. The tower spandrels are decorated with ornate central panels and horizontal line forms. The entire facade above ground level is clad in green faience tiles, chosen to match the colour of contemporary train carriages and a shade subsequently used for a period on all of Sydney's public transport including its ferries. Entered via Railway House, Wynyard station retains many original 1930s fittings including escalators with timber tread and veneer panelling manufactured by the Otis Company.

Shortly after opening, Railway House was awarded the Royal Australian Institute of Architects Sulman Award (1935) followed by a Royal Institute of British Architects Medal in 1939.

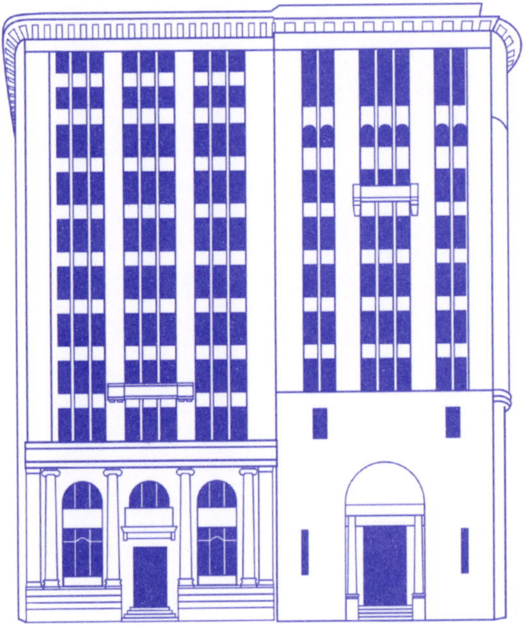

20 343 & 341 George St / 1925 & 1932 / Kent & Massie, Robertson & Marks

COMMERCIAL BANKING & BANK OF NSW BUILDINGS

Two of Australia's earliest financial institutions, the Commercial Banking Company of Sydney (est. 1834) and the Bank of NSW (est. 1817) had both occupied the block on George Street since the 1850s. Presenting an image of prosperity and confidence to the public was important in the years following the First World War and the CBC decided to achieve this by constructing a grand new headquarters at 343 George Street. A Commercial Palazzo-style building with clear classic motifs, the upper sandstone-clad levels sit above a base of rusticated stone. The George Street entrance is highlighted by four trachyte columns with Ionic capitals supporting an entablature engraved with the company name. Tall bronze-framed arch windows skirt the ground level whilst the sandstone facades are punctuated with bays of rectangular casement windows.

Abutting the CBC building is the equally impressive 1932 Bank of NSW. Constructed as a direct response to their business rival, the bank directed architects Robertson & Marks to design a building that matched the height and floor articulation of the neighbouring structure. Designed in a decoratively more restrained style, the George Street facade is dominated by the enormous arched entrance faced with grey rusticated stone. Within the arch the bank's coat of arms sits atop an entablature supported by red granite columns.

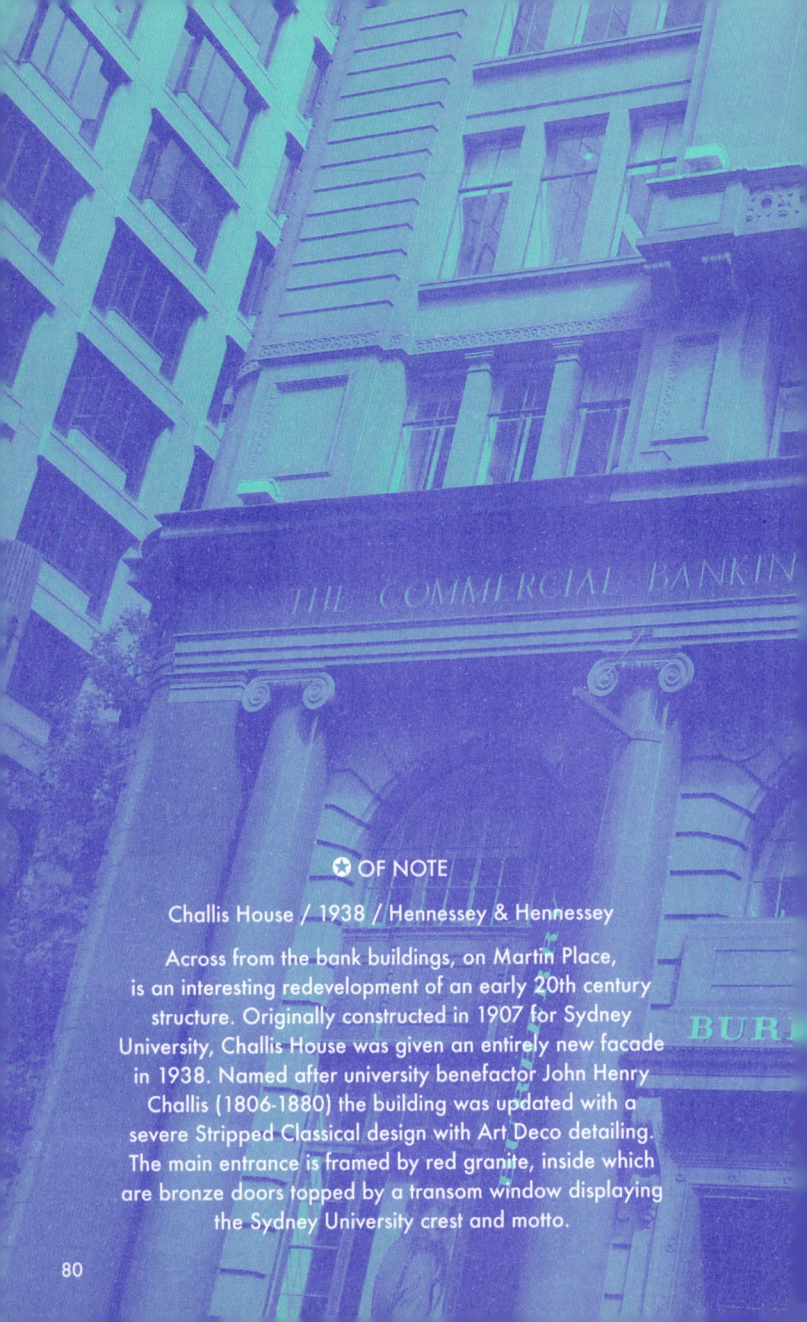

✪ OF NOTE

Challis House / 1938 / Hennessey & Hennessey

Across from the bank buildings, on Martin Place, is an interesting redevelopment of an early 20th century structure. Originally constructed in 1907 for Sydney University, Challis House was given an entirely new facade in 1938. Named after university benefactor John Henry Challis (1806-1880) the building was updated with a severe Stripped Classical design with Art Deco detailing. The main entrance is framed by red granite, inside which are bronze doors topped by a transom window displaying the Sydney University crest and motto.

A deliberate act of one upmanship between corporate rivals, the Bank of NSW building was widely criticised by contemporary architects and academics as clashing aesthetically with its neighbour and of cheekily "making its entrance look like the entrance to both buildings".

View at the end
of walk at Circular Quay

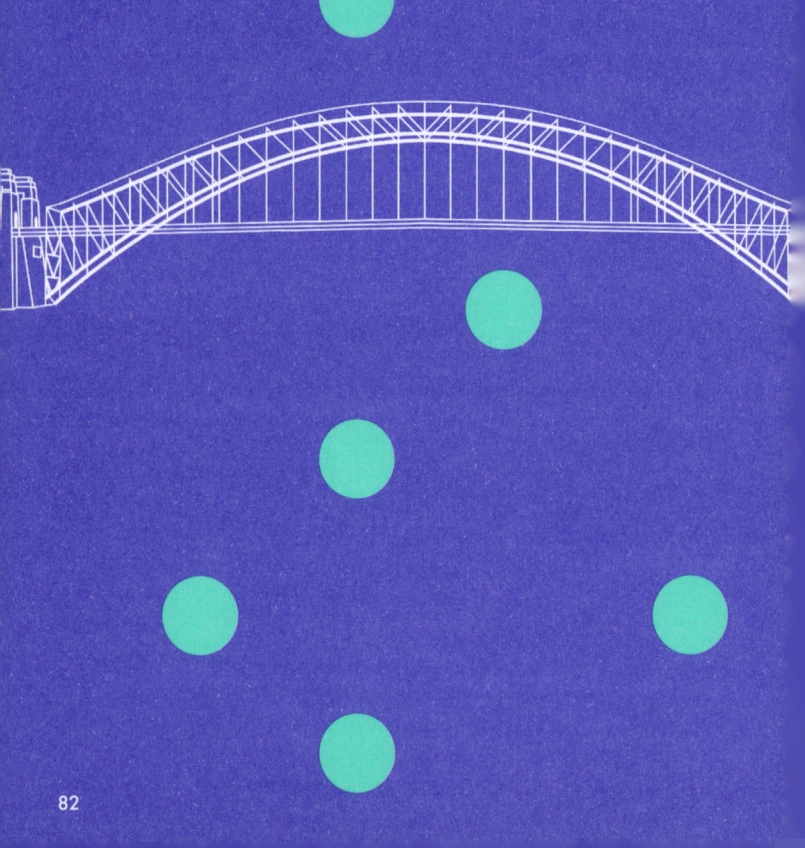

21 1932 / J. Bradfield and R. Freeman

SYDNEY HARBOUR BRIDGE

Nicknamed the "Coathanger" by locals, the Sydney Harbour Bridge is, along with the Opera House, the most recognisable built symbol of the city.

Plans to link the northern and southern shores of Sydney Harbour were first proposed by convict architect Francis Greenway in 1815. Many other suggestions were put forward throughout the 19th century but it wasn't until after the First World War that serious action was taken to design and construct a bridge. John Bradfield had been appointed Chief Engineer of Sydney Harbour Bridge and Metropolitan Railway Construction in 1914 and, following the war, began to develop ideas for a suitable structure. Initially favouring a cantilever design, Bradfield and his team eventually decided that a single arched bridge would be more suitable as it was both cheaper and offered more structural rigidity. Inspired by the Hells Gate Bridge in New York City (1916) the winning design, submitted via a 1923 tendering process, was produced by UK engineering firm Dorman Long and Company Ltd. Construction began in 1924 and was completed in January 1932 at a total cost of AU£6.25 million.

Stretching between Millers Point at the southern end and Milsons Point at the north, the main arch is composed of grey painted steel trusses and joists. The large towers at the each end of the span are concrete clad in granite quarried from Moruya, NSW. Although abutment structures at their bases support the arch loads, the towers themselves were designed for purely aesthetic reasons, serving no engineering purpose.

Dimensionally the bridge still holds its own internationally being the world's tallest single span arch bridge (134m) and the sixth longest (503m).

GEORGE RAYNOR HOFF

(1894 – 1937)

The son of a woodcarver and stonemason, George Raynor Hoff was born on the Isle of Man on 27 November 1894. Assisting his father on architectural projects from an early age, he went on to study drawing and design at Nottingham School of Art from 1910 to 1915. He enlisted in the British Army in 1915, was sent to France the following year and fought in the trenches before being transferred to a topographical survey unit. These experiences no doubt left an indelible mark on his psyche, reflected in the powerful pieces he later created for various war memorial projects.

After the war Hoff studied at the Royal College of Art under sculptor Francis Derwent Wood and in 1921 travelled to Rome on a scholarship. A meeting with Australian architect Hardy Wilson in Naples sparked a series of events that led to the young artist being appointed director of sculpture and drawing at East Sydney Technical College in May, 1923.

An energetic artist and administrator, Hoff sought to raise the profile of sculpture in Australia through the exhibition and promotion not only of his own work but that of his students.

Sculpting works in all scales (including numerous medal designs for various arts and industry awards) his most significant contributions to the medium were the large publicly visible pieces, especially those commissioned for war memorials.

Beginning with three bronze relief panels for the Dubbo Memorial (1925), Hoff was subsequently commissioned to design marble reliefs and bronze statues for the National War Memorial in Adelaide (1930) followed by extensive panels and sculptures for the Hyde Park ANZAC Memorial (1934). Although his artistic inspirations were broad, ranging from classical Graeco-Roman to Art Deco, the figures represented in these pieces appear neither excessively heroic nor superficially stylised; Hoff instead managed to embed in them a sense of nobility and humanity whilst still communicating the tragedy of the events depicted.

The dramatic centrepiece of the Hyde Park Memorial, 'Sacrifice', is a powerful symbol of the Great War's young victims, as truly understood and represented by Hoff, the veteran and artist.

Hoff died in 1937 of pancreatitis at the age of just 42.

Although now widely considered the most important sculptor working in Sydney during the inter-war years, most Australians are unknowingly aware of his work through the Holden car company. Designed by Hoff in 1928 the "lion and stone" logo, although altered slightly over the years, remains the corporate symbol of the firm.

INTER-WAR TIMELINE
1914–1939

1914 Outbreak of the First World War. Australia pledges full support to Britain after she declares war on Germany in August.

1915 The Gallipoli campaign begins with the landing of the Australian Imperial Forces (AIF) on Anzac Cove on 25 April.

1916 Taronga Zoo opens on 7 October. Taronga is an indigenous word meaning 'beautiful view'.

1918 The First World War ends with an armistace declared on 11 November, by which time over 60,000 Australian soldiers have been killed.

1921 Inaugural Archibald Prize (administered by trustees of the Art Gallery of NSW) is won by William McInnes for a portrait of architect H. Desbrowe Annear. Annear (1865-1933) was instrumental in the development of the Arts and Craft movement in Australia.

1922 Independent children's charity the Smith Family is founded in Sydney by five businessmen.

1923 First official radio station begins broadcasting in Sydney. Initially known as 2SB it is now 702 ABC Sydney, the flagship station in the ABC local radio network.

1924 First regular commercial flights begin operating from Sydney airport (Mascot).

1929 The Great Depression hits. Continuing construction of Sydney Harbour Bridge, begun in 1923, alleviates to some extent the unemployment crisis.

1932 The official opening of Sydney Harbour Bridge is famously disrupted by Francis De Groot, a member of right-wing royalist group the 'New Guard'. De Groot, mounted on horseback and wearing a military uniform, rides up and slashes the ceremonial opening ribbon with his sword.

1935 Luna Park, constructed at the foot of Sydney Harbour Bridge, opens 4 October.

1938 Sydney hosts the third British Empire Games from 5-12 February to coincide with Sydney's sesqui-centenary (150 years since the foundation of British settlement in Australia).

1939 Australia follows Britain in the declaration of war on Germany.

GLOSSARY

Art Deco: Taking its name from the 1925 Exposition Internationale des Arts Décoratifs et Industriels Modernes, the Art Deco style used vibrant colour and geometric shapes to express the speed and movement of industry and the Machine Age

Balconette: A false balcony created by a stone balustrade or cast iron railing framing the lower section of an upper floor window

Baroque: Elaborate, overly ornate decorative style originating in 17th century Italy

Buttress A structure of masonry or brick used to provide lateral support to a wall

Chamfered: A transitional edge between two facades of a building, usually a 45° angle

Chicagoesque: A style resulting from pioneering developments in the U.S (particularly Chicago) relating to steel frame engineering which enabled architects to design facades that expressed the inner structure, thereby creating larger window apertures. A precursor to the light curtain wall designs of the 1950s

Colonnade: A series of columns supporting an entablature

Commercial Palazzo: A style that utilized the form and proportions of Italian Renaissance palaces for late 19th and early 20th century commercial buildings

Coping: The capping or covering of a wall

Corinthian: One of the five classical orders, characterized by acanthus leaves decorating the capitals

Cornice: A continuous horizontal moulding crowning a building or aperture

Dentil: A small block used in repetition as a decorative feature on a cornice

Doric: One of the five classical orders, characterised by a plain square capital

Entablature: The structure above the capital comprising architrave, frieze and cornice

Facade: An exterior side of a building, often referring to the front

Faience: Glazed terracotta tiles used for architectural cladding

Federation Style: Encompassing various revival styles popular in England around 1890-1915 (including Queen Anne and Edwardian) Federation architecture utilised, amongst other elements, extensive brickwork and decorative roof features

Fenestration: The arrangement and design of windows in a building

Frieze: The central component of the entablature, often decorated with a relief design

Gable: The triangular part of a wall between the sloping faces of a pitched roof

Ionic: One of the five classical orders, characterised by a scroll-like ornament decorating the capital and often fluted shaft

Loggia: A covered exterior gallery enclosed on one side by arcades or colonnades.

Mansard: French style four-sided roof

Mullion: A vertical form dividing a window

Parapet: A vertical extension of the facade wall at the edge of a roof

Pediment: A classical triangular shaped structure placed above the entablature of a building

Pier: An upright element or section providing structural support

Pilasters: A column feature projecting from the face of a wall (as opposed to a freestanding column)

Portico: A porch extending from the main body of a building

Quoin: Cornerstones of a wall, often rusticated.

Rustication: A masonry technique used to accentuate the joins between stone blocks. The face of each block is also often given a rough or patterned finish to further delineate each stone

Second Empire: Late 19th/early 20th century architecture inspired by that of the 2nd French Empire (1852 to 1870). Includes features such as Classic motifs, Baroque detailing and Mansard roofs.

Skyscraper Gothic: A Neo-Gothic style that applied soaring, vertical cathedral-like forms to skyscraper architecture.

Soffits: The underside of an architectural structure such as an awning or balcony

Solomonic column: A column with a spiral or twisting shaft

Spandrel: The space between the top of a window and the sill of the window in the storey above

Streamline Moderne: A late Art Deco style that emphasised horizontal lines and curved forms relating to vehicular movement

Stripped Classical: Inter-war architecture presenting classic architectural forms devoid of most or all ornamentation

Terrazzo: A flooring material composed of chips of marble, quartz, granite or glass, mixed with a binder and applied to the surface

Voussoir: A wedge-shaped element that forms part of an arch

Ziggurat: A terraced step pyramid form associated with ancient Middle Eastern architecture

THE WALK

The Footpath Guide to Inter-War architecture in Sydney takes approximately two hours to complete.

CONTENTS

3	Architectural Beginnings
7	Introduction
15	MSB Building
19	Cadmans Cottage
23	The Orient Hotel
27	The Rocks Police Station
33	British Seamen's Hotel
35	Susannah Place Museum
39	The Australian Hotel
43	The Argyle Cut
45	Sydney Observatory
47	Old Fort Street School
49	Kent Street Walk
51	Lord Nelson Hotel
55	Walsh Bay Wharves
57	Hero of Waterloo Hotel
61	The Garrison Church
63	Workers Flats
65	Clydebank
69	The Mercantile Hotel
71	Australasian Steam Navigation Company
77	Observer Hotel
80	Francis Greenway
82	The Rocks Timeline
86	Glossary

N

W

E

S

ARCHITECTURAL BEGINNINGS

When Captain Arthur Phillip sailed into Botany Bay, on the east coast of Australia, in January 1788, he was unimpressed. The bay was unprotected and shallow and surrounded by poor soil and its shore was observed to be unproductive with scarce fresh water. Having led a fleet of ships halfway around the world to found a penal colony for British convicts, he decided to explore further north for a better location.

He found it just 12 kilometres up the coast. Port Jackson was an inlet discovered and named by Captain James Cook in 1770 although it was not extensively explored at the time. What Phillip found as he ventured up the inlet was, in his opinion, 'the finest harbour in the world'.

Named after the British Home Secretary Thomas Townshend (Lord Sydney), Sydney Cove was a well sheltered deep water anchorage with ample fresh water supplies. It was a perfect site for the first official British settlement on the Australian continent.

FOR THE FIRST TWO DECADES OF SYDNEY'S EXISTENCE THE COLONY WAS SO LACKING IN APPROPRIATE SKILLS AND TOOLS THAT THE MAJORITY OF BUILDINGS CONSTRUCTED WERE OF POOR QUALITY AND IN NEED OF CONSTANT MAINTENANCE.

The situation changed dramatically with the appointment of Major-General Lachlan Macquarie as Governor of New South Wales in 1810. Finding many structures throughout the settlement in a 'most ruinous state of decay', Macquarie implemented a set of building codes that dictated a minimum standard for any future construction. Teaming up with convicted forger and architect Francis Greenway, the Governor also commissioned a series of classically inspired public buildings including Hyde Park Barracks (1819) and St James Church (1824), both of which still stand today.

From the mid to late 19th century architectural trends in Sydney closely followed those adopted throughout the British Empire. Grand classical revival styles were used extensively for public and administrative buildings whilst well to do residents displayed their wealth with elaborate Victorian Italianate or sober Georgian home designs.

6

INTRODUCTION

The Rocks area of Sydney, named in reference to the local sandstone deposits from which many early buildings were constructed, is an architecturally unique enclave.

Located near the CBD of Australia's largest city, The Rocks has managed to avoid widespread re-development over the past 50 years and, as a result, possesses many well preserved commercial and residential structures dating from the 19th and early 20th centuries.

Located on the southern shore of Sydney Harbour the area now known as The Rocks had been inhabited by native Gadigal people of the Eora nation for centuries before European settlement. Shortly after the British colony of Sydney was established in 1788 numerous dwellings began to appear, although the majority were poorly built timber or brick structures.

{ The local abundant sandstone provided the material for many new buildings throughout the following decades, from the oldest residential structure, Cadmans Cottage (1816), to the former Maritime Services Board building (1952), currently the Museum of Contemporary Art. }

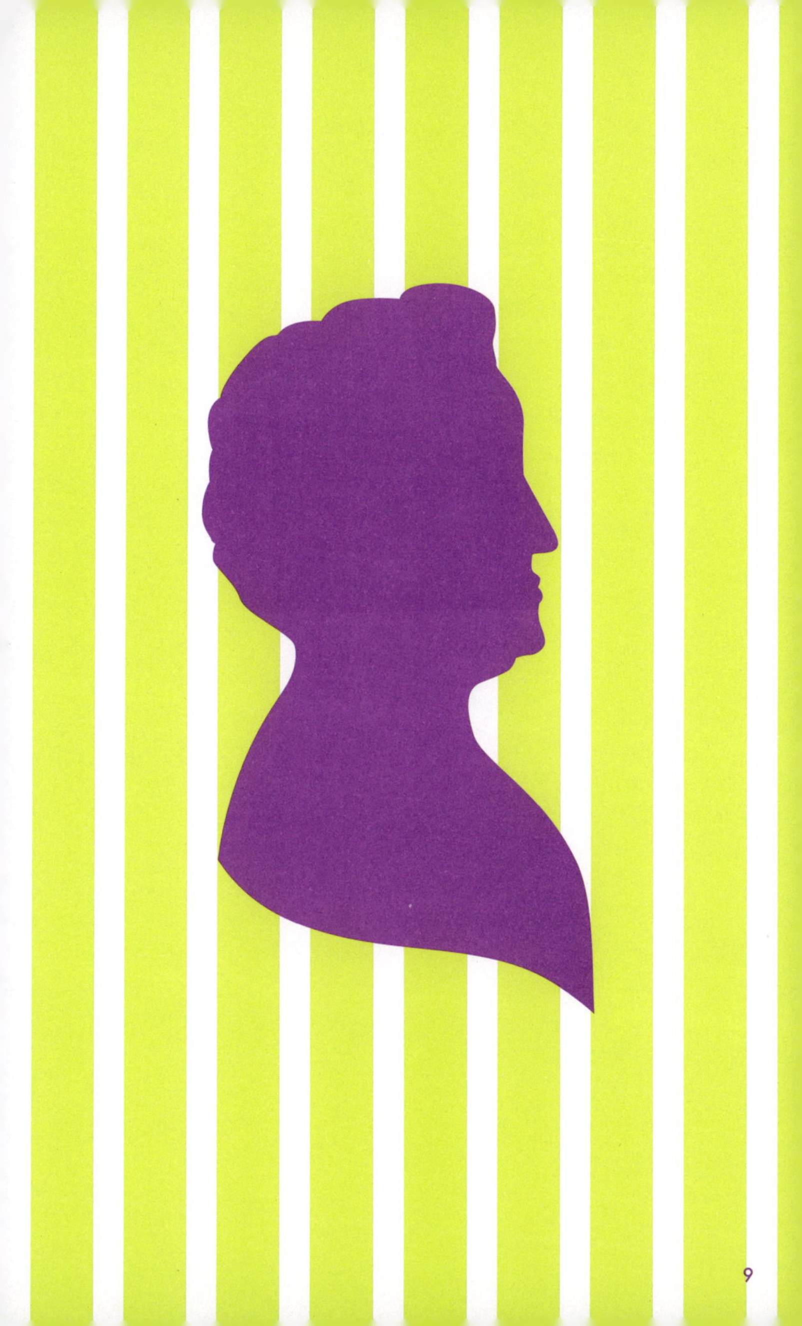

For much of its existence The Rocks area, being typical of many port settlements, was notorious for the various nefarious activities that patrons of its numerous taverns and brothels engaged in, particularly along the waterfront. By the end of the 19th century many residents were living in slum conditions. After an outbreak of bubonic plaque in 1900 the NSW Government took control of the area, and proceeded to demolish hundreds of dwellings ostensibly to pave the way for better housing conditions.

The building of Sydney Harbour Bridge (1923) and the Cahill Expressway (1955-57) resulted in the loss of many more buildings and it was not until the 1970s that widespread concern was raised about the disappearance of much of The Rocks early built heritage.

Passionate community based activism and trade union supported 'green bans' (a form of strike action for environmental or conservation purposes) eventually resulted in widespread protection and heritage listing of many significant Rocks buildings.

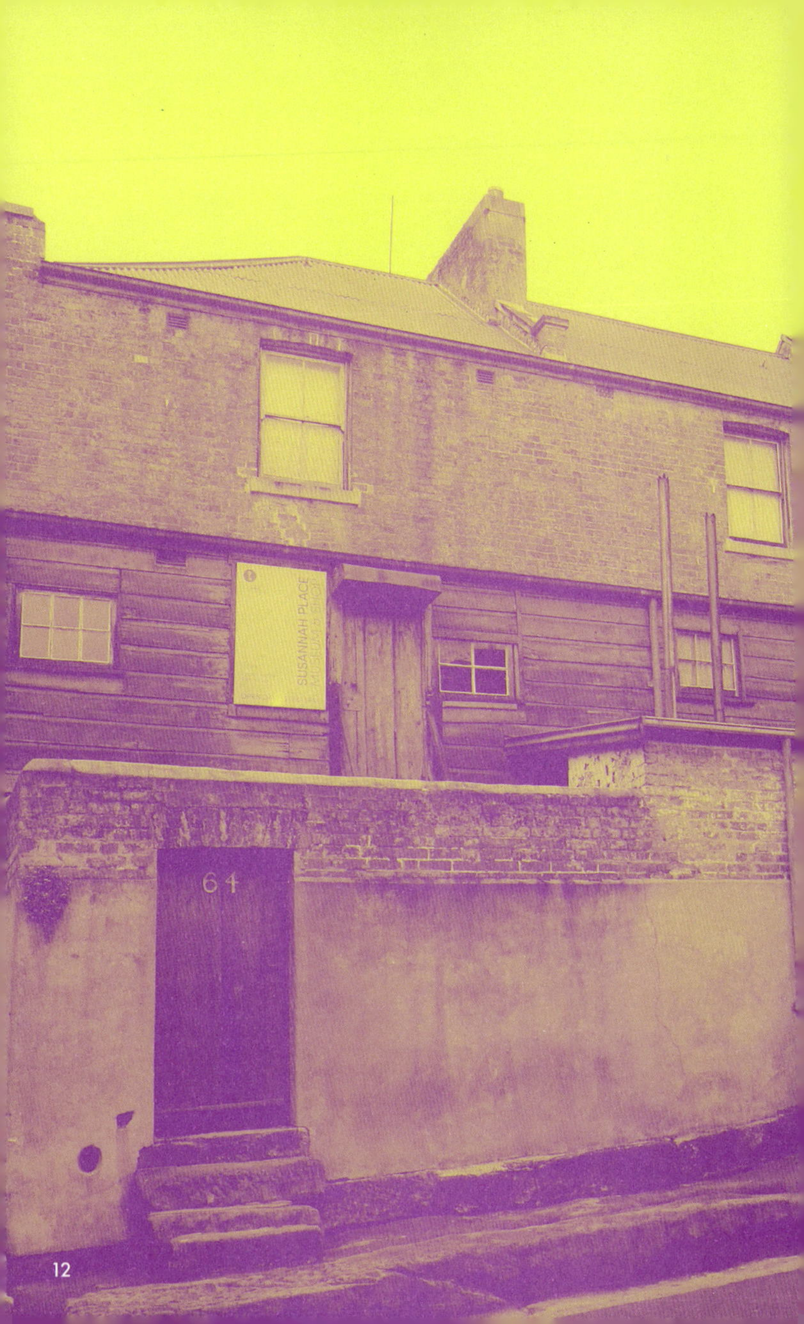
SUSANNAH PLACE
64

Today The Rocks, through its architecture, provides a rich and varied glimpse into the development of the city of Sydney, from settlement through to the first half of the 20th century.

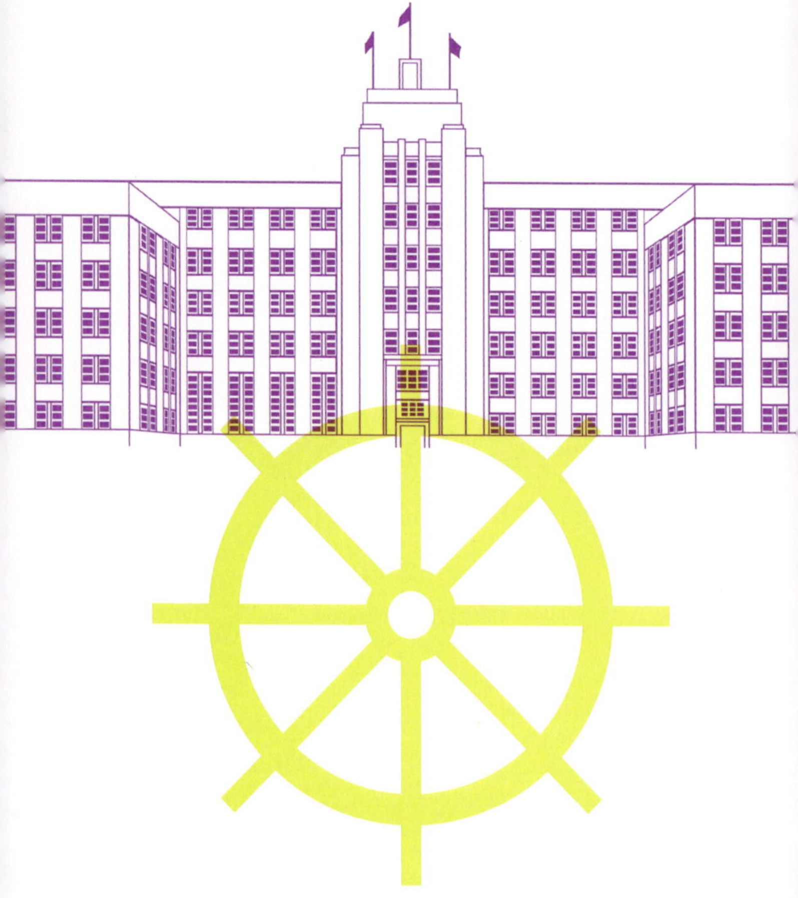

1 Circular Quay West / 1952 / W.D.H Baxter

MSB BUILDING

Previously known as the Sydney Harbour Trust, by 1936 the organisation responsible for all NSW commercial and recreational marine activities had been renamed the Maritime Services Board and was in the process of relocating its offices. The site chosen had been occupied by the Commissariat Stores, built by convict labour, from 1809. By 1939 the buildings had been demolished and plans drawn up in preparation for the construction of the new MSB premises. World War Two intervened, however, and it was not until 1949 that the foundation stone was laid.

By the time it was completed in 1952 the new building's heavy stripped classical exterior and art deco interiors were considered old fashioned, especially compared to the emerging post-war Modernist styles. It is nonetheless a fine example of inter-war styled administrative architecture, built around a steel and concrete frame with yellow Maroubra sandstone-faced walls. The severe symmetry of the 'H' plan office is emphasised by the central tower with its expressed vertical elements and polished granite framed entrance. External decoration is limited to a bas-relief above the entrance doors and sandstone carvings of a ship's propeller, wheel and anchor below the tower clock. Internally there is extensive use of polished Wombeyan and green marble in addition to much decorative maritime-themed metalwork.

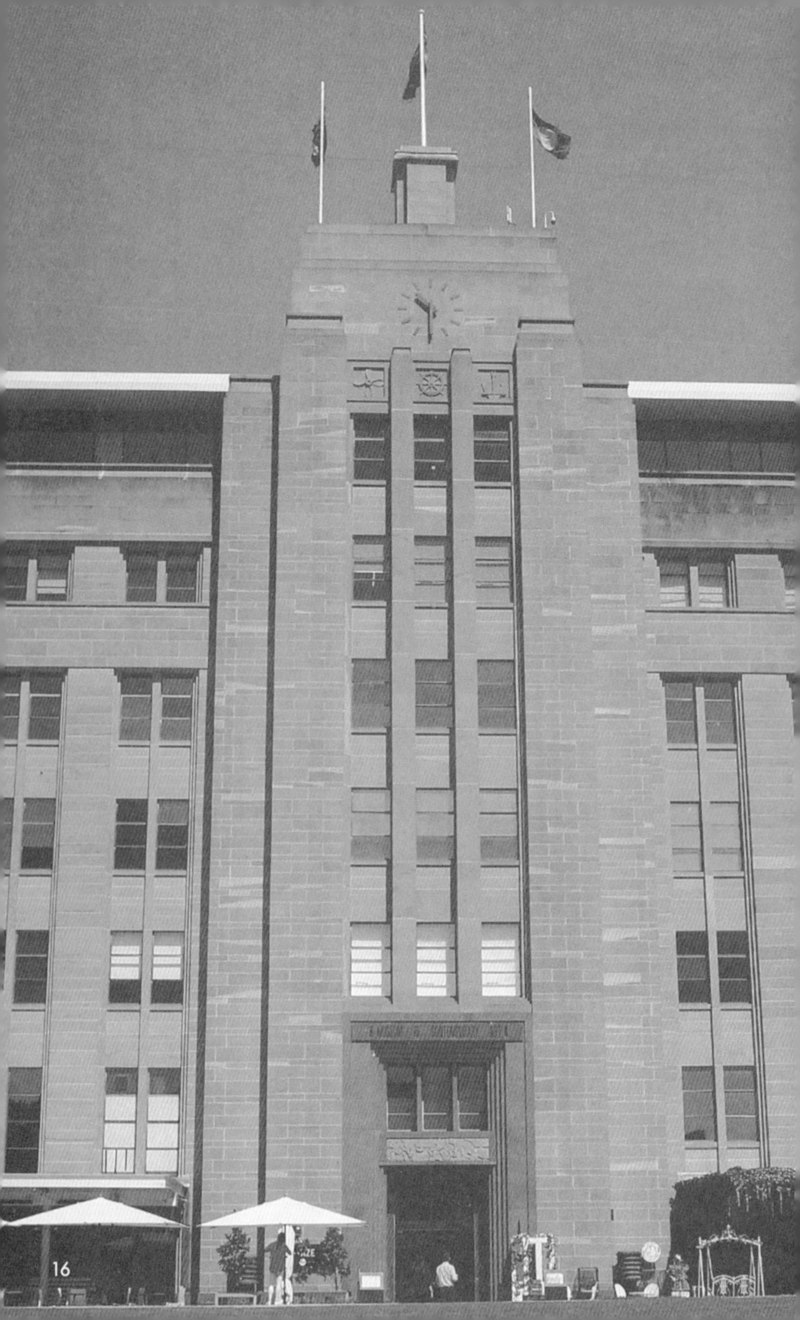

The MSB moved to a CBD location in 1989 and the Circular Quay building has, since 1991, been home to the Museum of Contemporary Art.

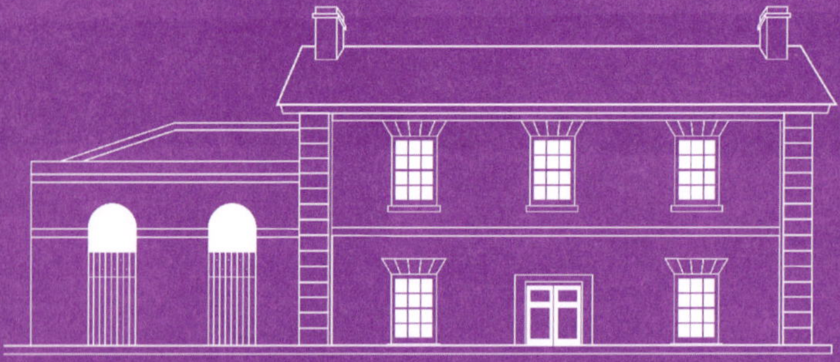

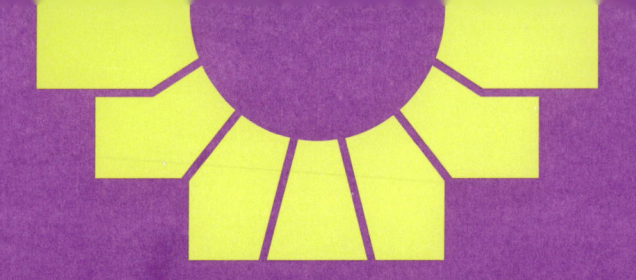

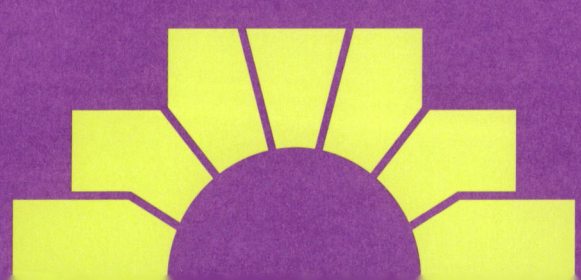

2 110 George St / 1816 / Francis Greenway

CADMANS COTTAGE

In 1798 convict John Cadman arrived in Sydney having been found guilty of stealing a horse in Bewdley, Worcestershire. Working as a coxswain on a government boat from 1809 he was given a free pardon by Governor Macquarie in 1821 and went on to be master of the Cutter 'Mars' four years later. In 1827 he was promoted to the post of Superintendent of Government Boats and moved into the rough stone cottage on The Rocks shoreline with his family.

The cottage had been home to three previous Government coxswains but is now known by the name of its last and longest serving resident, the position being abolished after Cadman's retirement in 1845. Constructed in 1816 of sandstone in a simple Colonial Georgian style, the cottage has been used over the years as headquarters of the Sydney Water Police (1845-64) and the Sydney Sailors Home (1865-1970).

Restoration began in 1972 shortly after heritage listing (as Sydney's oldest residential structure) and the cottage is now open to the public, serving as the Sydney Harbour National Park Information Centre.

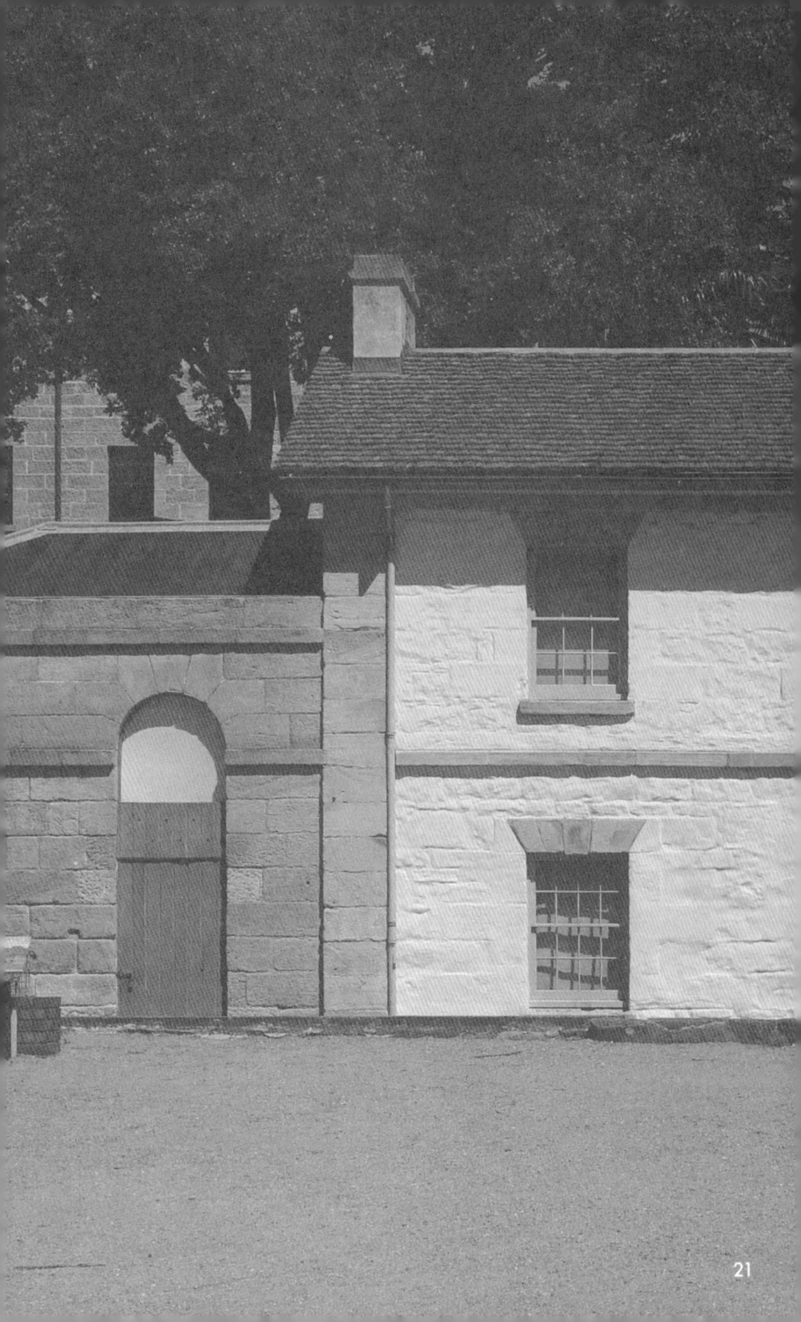

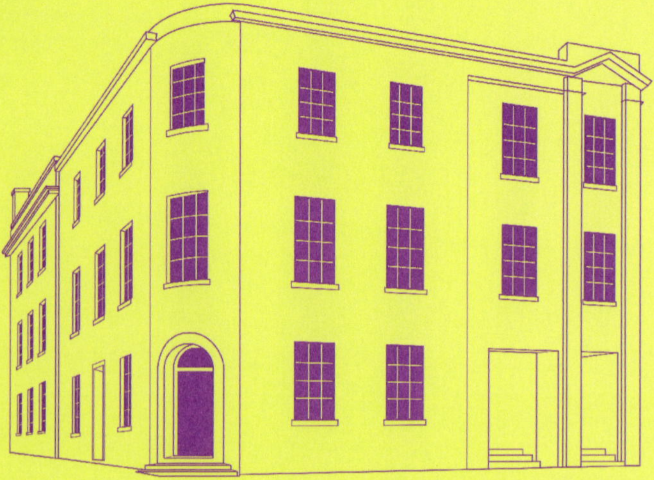

3 89 George St / 1844 / James Chapman

THE ORIENT HOTEL

The site on which the Orient Hotel is located was once part of Sydney's first hospital complex, founded shortly after the First Fleet landed in 1788. The land was subdivided in 1841 and lots 1 and 2 were purchased by butcher James Chapman who, in 1842, proceeded to construct a three-storey, ten-room residence and an adjoining single-storey shop. By the time of Chapman's death in 1856 the residence had been converted to a licensed premises named the Marine Hotel. Witnessing a succession of owners and publicans, as well as name changes, over the years, the hotel has been known as the Orient since 1885 when it was purchased by Walter McCombie. The name was possibly inspired by the fact that from 1877 ships of the Orient Steam Navigation Line berthed at the nearby, newly developed Campbell's Wharf.

By the 1930s the original single-storey shop and subsequent shed structures had been demolished to make way for extensions to both the Argyle and George Street facades. These additions closely matched the building's Colonial Georgian style with its plain walls, rectangular windows and curved corner facade.

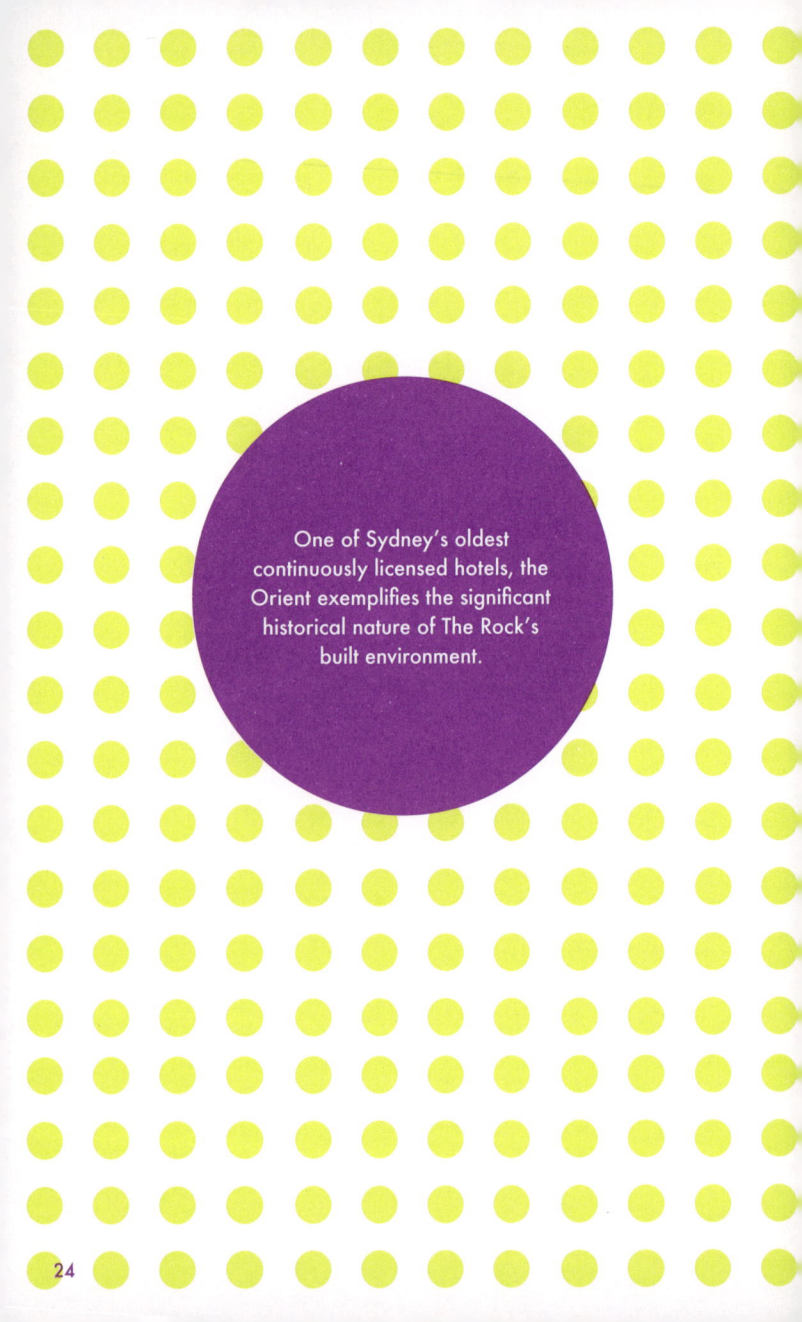

One of Sydney's oldest continuously licensed hotels, the Orient exemplifies the significant historical nature of The Rock's built environment.

ORIENT
1844
HOTEL
RESTAURANT
SEAFOOD
STEAK
ORIENT HOTEL
NO
ENTRY
EMERGENCY
VEHICLES
EXCEPTED
NO
STOPPING
LOADING
ZONE
ORIENT
HOTEL
RESTAURANT

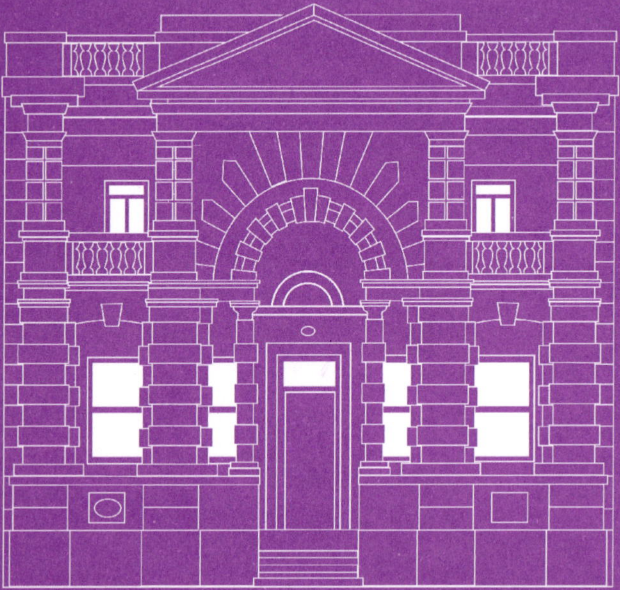

4 127 George St / 1882 / James Barnet

THE ROCKS POLICE STATION

As official Colonial Architect for NSW (1862-90) James Barnet designed numerous classically inspired public buildings including the General Post Office (1891) and the Department of Lands building (1893). His smaller projects included 155 police stations located throughout the state, of which The Rocks building is surely the most elaborate. The two-storey facade, comprising a central arched entrance flanked by single window bays, resembles a Palladian-inspired water gate (a structure allowing easy, dry access from a quay or harbour to a castle or town wall). Many elements, including the piers, quoins and voussoirs, are heavily articulated, lending a highly textured quality to the surface.

Within the pediment above the arch are the initials VR (Victoria Regina), referring to Queen Victoria, whilst the arch's keystone displays a carved lion's head (representing British justice) holding a policeman's truncheon in its mouth. Currently made of hardwood the original truncheon was possibly bronze but, as a result of previous thefts, has been replaced on numerous occasions.

The building operated as No. 4 Police Station until 1974, briefly serving as a U.S. Navy lock up during the Second World War. Currently occupied by a café, the structure is a distinctive and intact example of a 19th century Victorian metropolitan police station, retaining many of the architectural details that identify its specific role.

✪ OF NOTE

Hospital plaque (former Rocks police station)

Located below the left ground level window bay of the police station is a plaque commemorating the site of Sydney's first hospital. Established as a series of tents soon after the First Fleet arrived in 1788, it soon developed into a more substantial complex of timber and brick structures boasting a well-equipped laboratory and dispensary. Further enhanced by a prefabricated portable hospital that arrived with the Second Fleet in 1790, the facility eventually covered an area bounded by Globe, George, Harrington and Argyle Streets. It was replaced in 1816 by a new hospital (Sydney Hospital, which remains in operation) on Macquarie Street.

✪ OF NOTE

Suez Canal (1840s)

Running between George and Harrington Streets, the Suez Canal (thought to be a pun on the word 'sewers') is a rare original 19th century laneway with a notorious reputation. Brothels, opium dens and sly grog shops once satisfied the vices of those who dared to venture into the seedy thoroughfare.

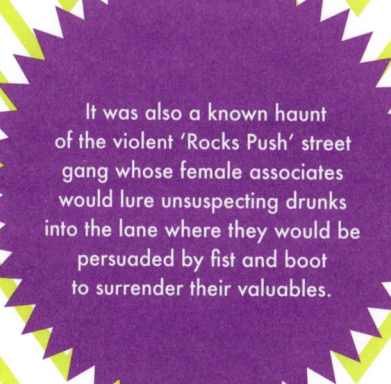

It was also a known haunt of the violent 'Rocks Push' street gang whose female associates would lure unsuspecting drunks into the lane where they would be persuaded by fist and boot to surrender their valuables.

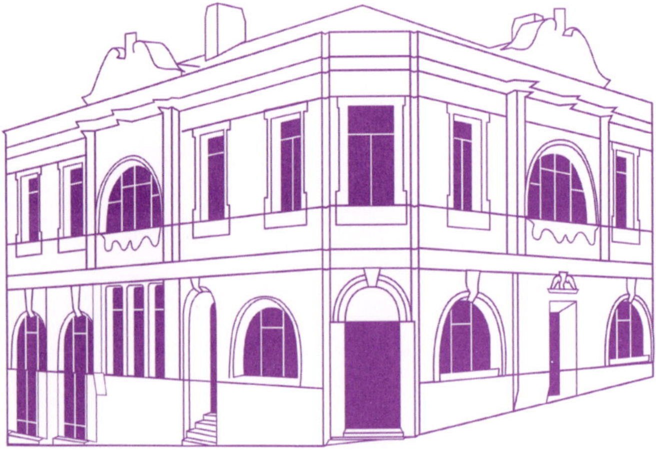

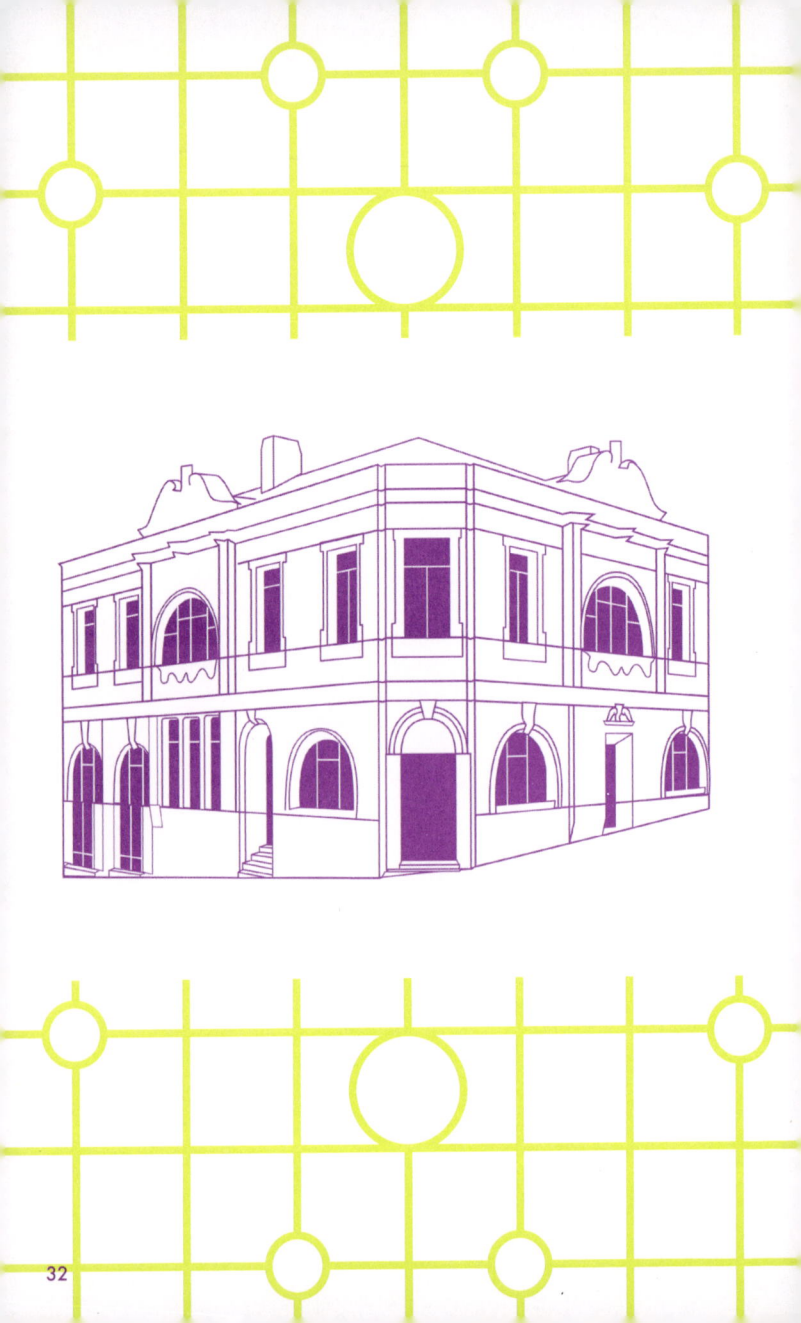

5 39-43 Argyle St / 1886

BRITISH SEAMEN'S HOTEL

When graziers John and William Gill opened their newly-built licenced premises in 1886 they retained the name of the hotel that had previously existed on the site. In fact, a public house of some kind had operated there since 1830 when Caleb Slater became innkeeper of what was then known as the 'Kings Head'.

The British Seamen's Hotel is an early example of what is now referred to as Federation Queen Anne, an Australian take on a style that became popular in the U.K from the late 19th century. Emerging as part of the Arts and Crafts movement this revival style utilised picturesque motifs and materials inspired by romantic notions of pre-industrial architecture. In this case the style is expressed in the building's alternating facade treatment of rendered banding and brickwork, scrolled pediments and arched, multi-casement windows. Additional decorative flourishes include bands of floral themed motifs below the second-storey arch windows and dentil courses under the cornices, both of which became frequently applied features of Australian hotel architecture after Federation (1901).

From 1899 the pub was known as the Hughes's Family Hotel, before becoming McCarthy's Hotel in the 1920s. Around 1928 the building became a boarding house, then offices until major conservation work was undertaken in 1995 resulting in a highly original exterior and interior.

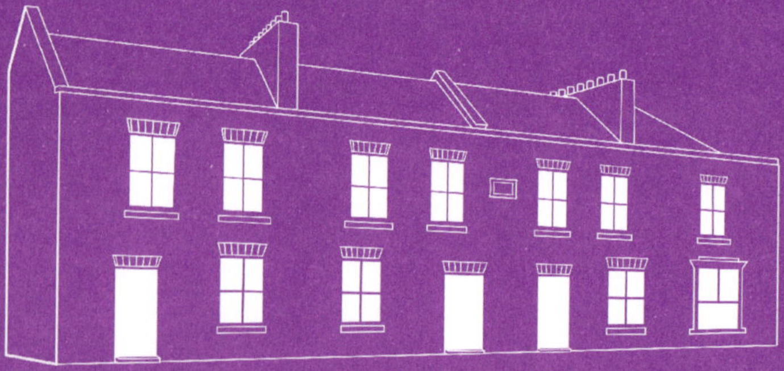

6 58-64 Gloucester St / 1844

SUSANNAH PLACE MUSEUM

Continuously occupied for almost 150 years, the four terrace houses that make up Susannah Place offer a rare insight into domestic working class life in The Rocks throughout the 19th and 20th centuries. They were built by Edward Riley who, along with his wife Mary and their niece Susannah (after whom the terraces were named), lived in number 62 for nearly 30 years whilst leasing out numbers 58, 60 and 64 to a variety of tenants. Riley and his family arrived in Sydney in 1838 as assisted immigrants, somehow finding the means to purchase the land on Gloucester Street just four years later, in the midst of a depression, for the substantial sum of 450 pounds.

The terraces are constructed of colonial bond brickwork (where the bricks are laid in alternating rows of stretcher and header configuration) on a sandstone foundation. Simply detailed and proportioned, each three-level terrace originally comprised six rooms with a basement kitchen and outhouses. The original shingle roof, surrounded by a sandstone-capped parapet, was replaced with corrugated iron in the late 19th century.

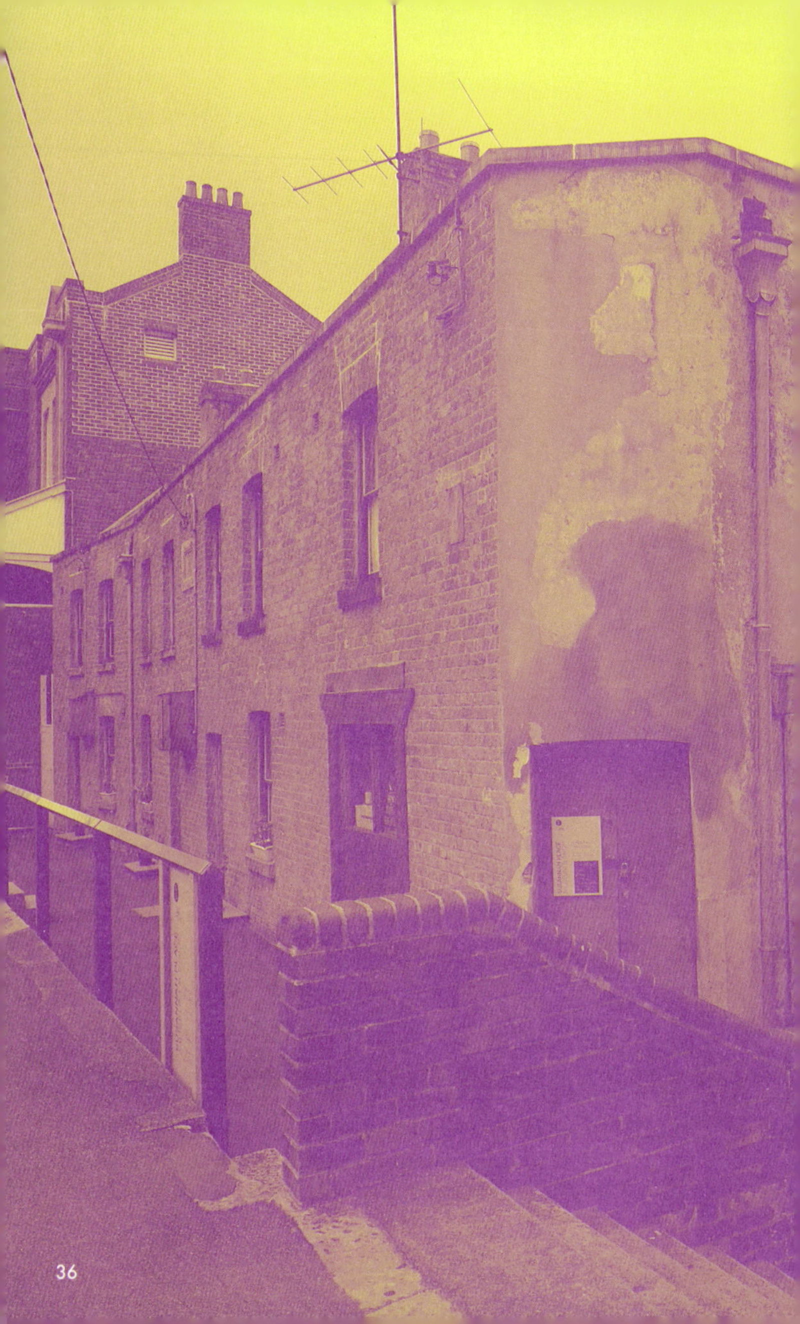

The last tenants,
Ellen and Dennis Marshall,
moved out of number 62 in 1990.
In 1992, after extensive restoration work,
the terraces were put in the hands of the
Historic Houses Trust of NSW and opened
as a museum. Visitors enter through
number 64, the corner terrace
which operated as a shop
until 1935.

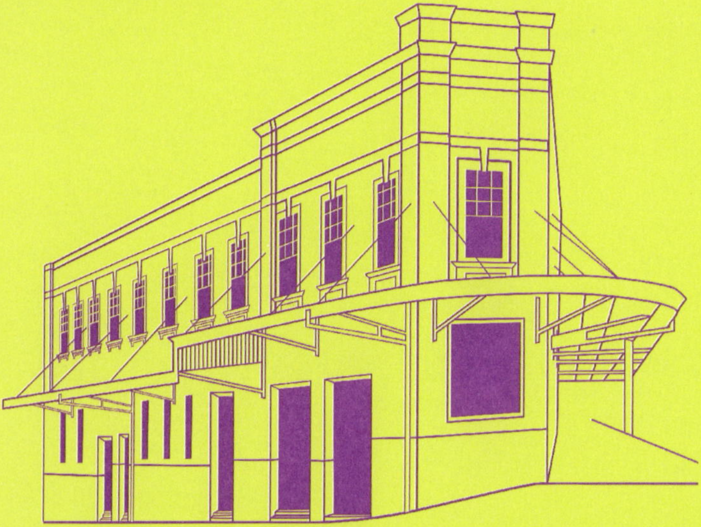

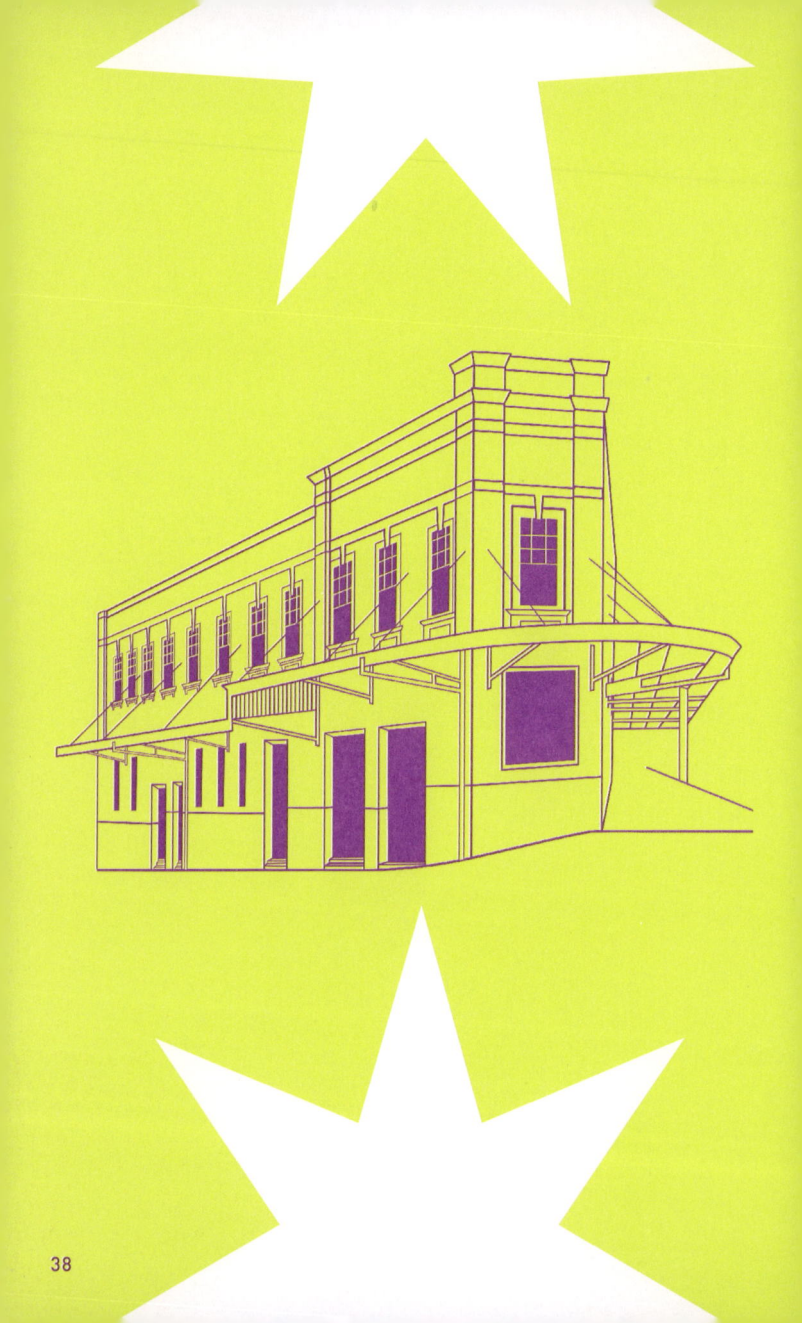

7 100 Cumberland St / 1914

THE AUSTRALIAN HOTEL

Sited prominently on a street corner, the Australian Hotel replaced a pub of the same name that had been demolished due to the realignment of Cumberland Street around 1907. Designed in an Italianate style the two-storey structure is rendered brick (partially exposed at the first level) punctuated by tall rectangular windows and topped by a stepped parapet.

Subtle moulded banding decorates the upper facade which was repainted in original 1920s colours during extensive conservation works in 1991-92. The interior, with its unique split level bar, is relatively intact with many original fittings and decorative features.

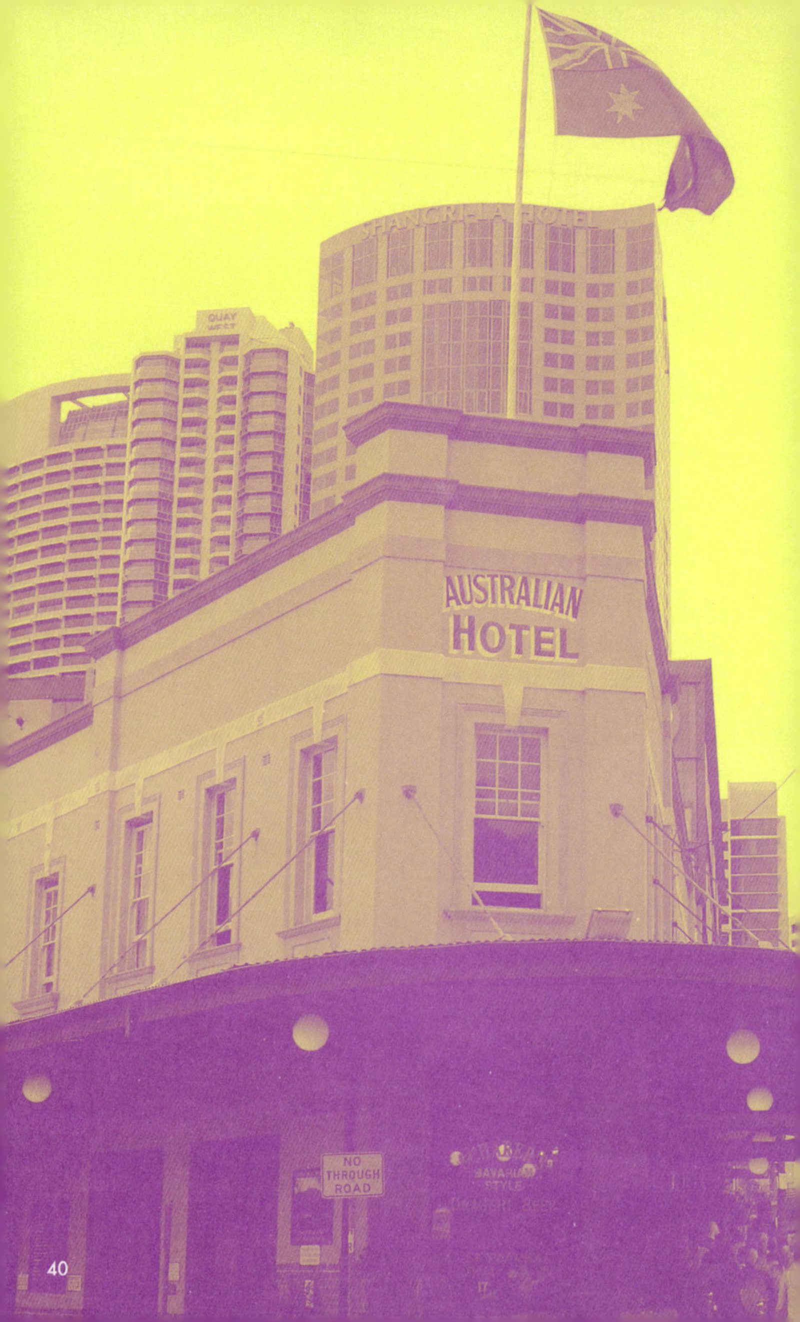
QUAY WEST
AUSTRALIAN HOTEL
NO THROUGH ROAD

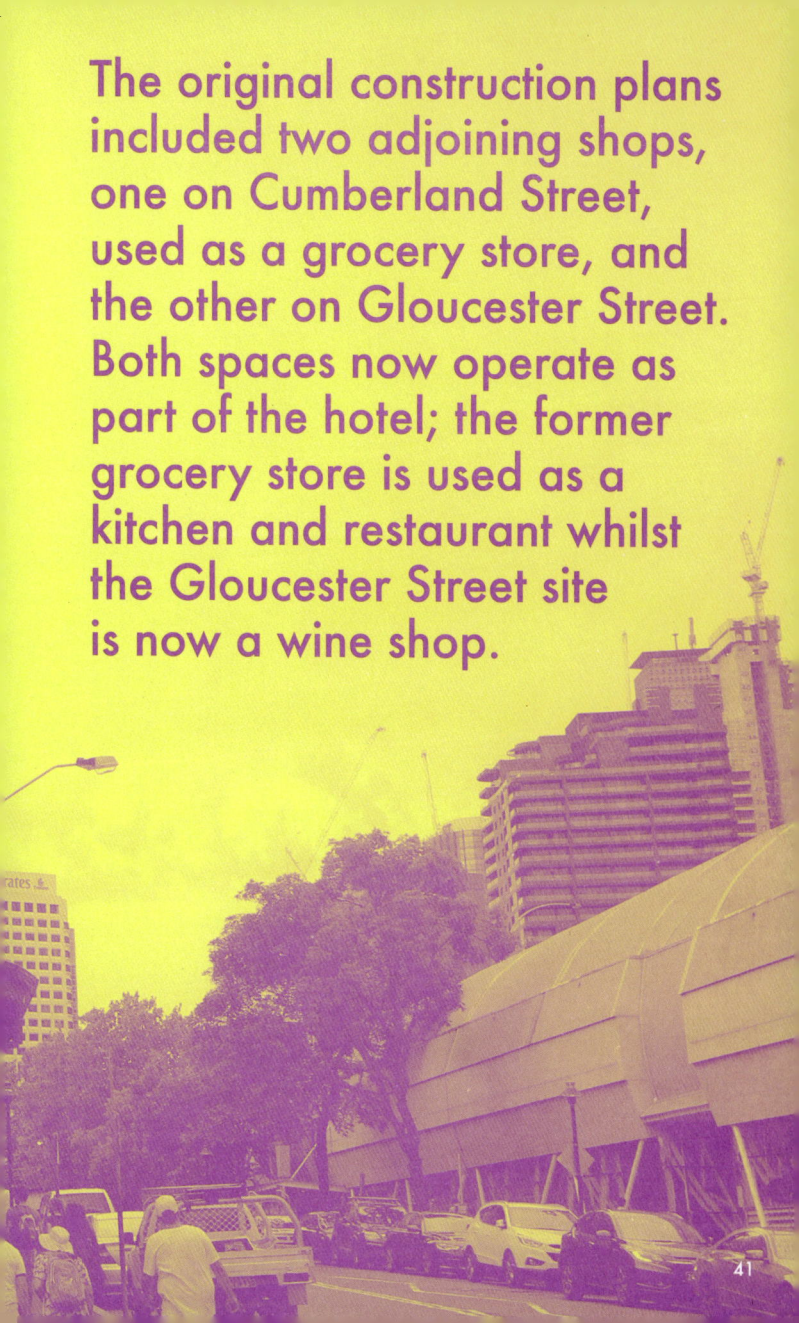

The original construction plans included two adjoining shops, one on Cumberland Street, used as a grocery store, and the other on Gloucester Street. Both spaces now operate as part of the hotel; the former grocery store is used as a kitchen and restaurant whilst the Gloucester Street site is now a wine shop.

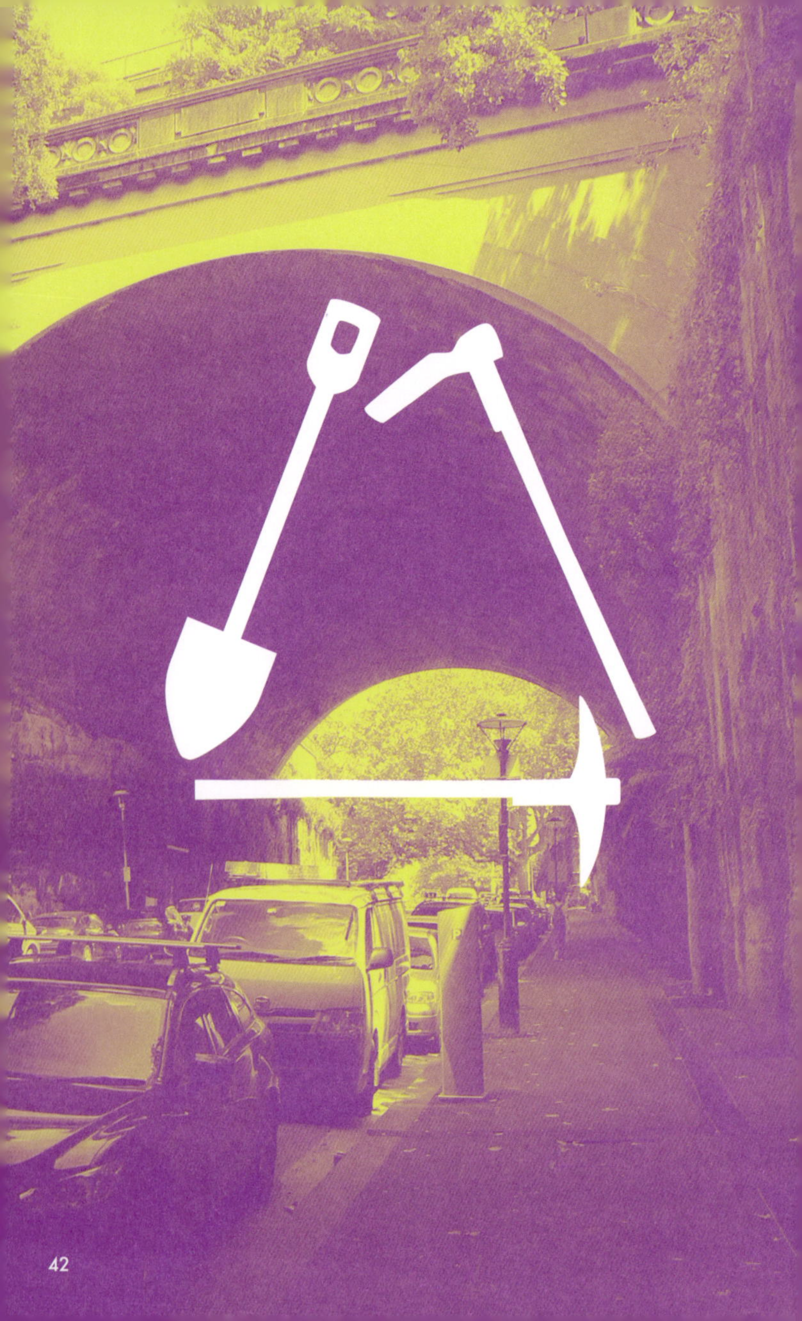

8 Argyle St / 1843-68

THE ARGYLE CUT

As the settlement of Sydney grew throughout the early 19th century increasing demands were made to improve access between The Rocks and Millers Point. The natural sandstone barrier dividing the two areas was a serious impediment to both the transport and mercantile activities that were increasing at an enormous pace, especially after the development of Darling Harbour. Vehicles travelling between Sydney Cove and Darling Harbour had to negotiate a convoluted route whilst pedestrians braved a crudely made and rapidly deteriorating set of stairs cut into the rock.

Wealthy landowner and merchant Alexander Berry put forward a proposal for a cutting, intending to profit from the project by creating it as a toll road. Governor Richard Bourke, however, decided that the project should be undertaken by the government and, in 1832, Governor Bourke instructed architect Edward Hallen to prepare plans. Work began in 1843, undertaken by convict labour under the harsh supervision of Tim Lane who motivated the workers with inspirational statements such as 'by the help of God and the strong arm of the flogger, you'll get fifty before breakfast tomorrow!' It was soon apparent, however, that the task was beyond simple hand tools and the cut was finally completed in 1859 by Sydney Municipal Council with the aid of explosives and better skilled council workers.

Around 1912 the Argyle Stairs (Arched entrance, on the right when facing west up Argyle Street) were constructed to link Argyle Street with Gloucester (Gloucester Walk) and Cumberland Streets.

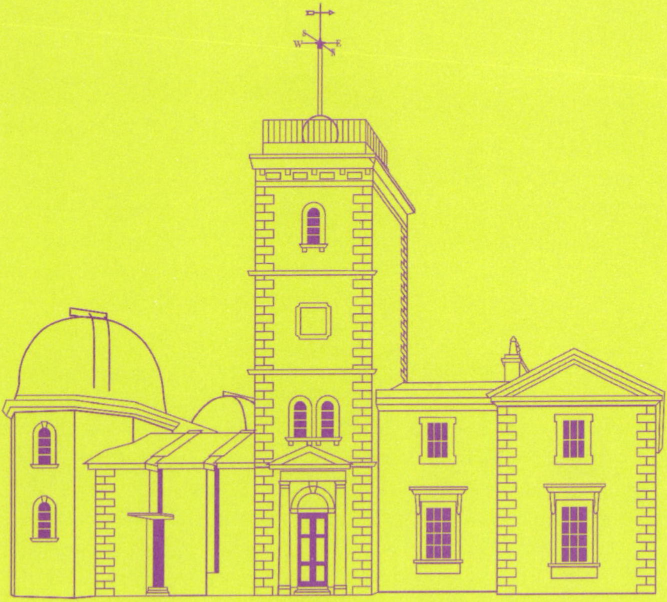

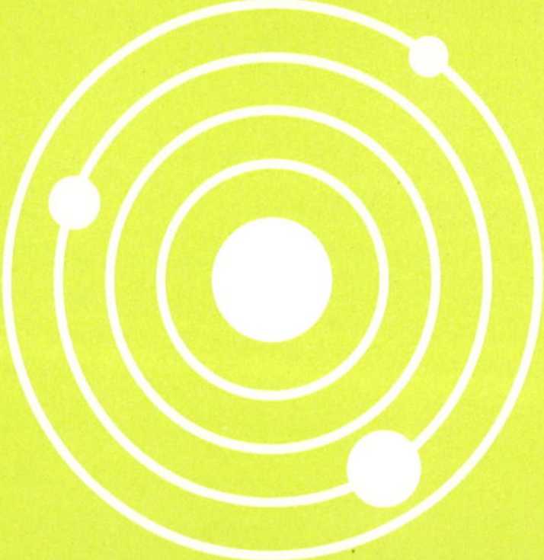

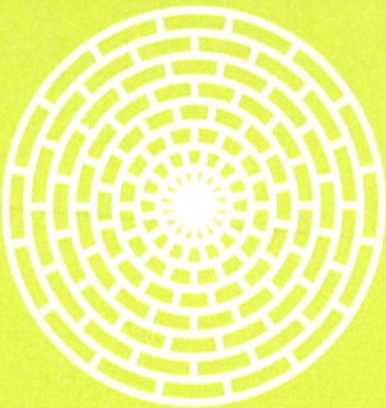

9 Watson Rd / 1858 / Alexander Dawson

SYDNEY OBSERVATORY

Located on what is appropriately known as Observatory Hill, the present structure was the third such facility to be established in the colony. The first was set up on Dawes Point soon after the arrival of the First Fleet in order to observe a comet that was calculated to appear in 1790. A second observatory was built in Parramatta in 1821 by Governor Sir Thomas Brisbane but it was closed in 1847 due to neglect of the facilities by its superintendent.

Plans were drawn up for a third observatory in 1850 but it wasn't until 1857 that construction commenced. Completed in 1859, the two-storey sandstone structure is Italianate in style with a campanile-like tower. Floors are externally expressed with string courses and the corners feature articulated quoins which, along with the window surrounds and eaves, display fine stone workmanship. In 1874 the original south telescope dome was replaced with a larger copper clad structure to accommodate a newly acquired German Schroeder telescope which can still be seen today. The second dome, along with the west wing, was added in 1876. Initially the prime purpose of the new building was to be time keeping using a time ball mechanism. This can be seen atop the tower and is still in use, though for historical rather than practical reasons. Every day at 1:00pm the ball is dropped and then raised again via an electric motor, as opposed to manually as was the case originally.

✪ OF NOTE

Agar Steps (c1870)

Named after Thomas Agar, a well-known resident of The Rocks area, the Agar Steps were constructed to form a link between Observatory Hill and Kent Street. Comprised of 108 steps they overlook the former Kent Street Quarry and are considered the best surviving example of stairways providing access from the hill to the lower Rocks precinct.

10 Upper Fort St / 1815

OLD FORT STREET SCHOOL

The New South Wales Marine Corps was a volunteer unit created to guard convicts on the ships of the First Fleet. In 1792 it was replaced by the New South Wales Corps, an infamous regiment which later earned the nickname the "Rum Corps" due to its liquor trading monopoly. Initially housed in tents, the regiment constructed its proper military barracks in Wynyard and, in 1815, Governor Macquarie commissioned a military hospital to provide medical services for the soldiers.

The barracks moved in 1848 to Paddington and the hospital was converted for use as a government run, non-denominational school, the first such institution in the country. Initially called the Model School it was later known as Fort Street High School.

Constructed in rendered brick the building is Colonial Georgian in style overlaid with Classical Revival features. The two-storey symmetrical facade is decorated with three separate entablature forms supported by eight pilasters, each of which is topped by a Corinthian capital. The Royal coat of arms of the United Kingdom sits above the central entablature. The arched windows were originally unglazed forming open loggias on both levels.

Co-educational from the beginning, due to increasing student numbers the male students moved to new premises in Petersham in 1916 whilst the girls remained at Fort Street until 1975. The building now operates as the NSW headquarters of the National Trust.

11 Kent St / 1810

KENT STREET WALK

Following the Agar Steps down will place you on Kent Street, one of the longest streets in Sydney. Running north-south between Walsh Bay and Darling Harbour, it was named in 1810 by Governor Macquarie in honour of the Duke of Kent, the younger brother of King George III.

The eastern side of the street, between the Agar Steps and Argyle Street, was once known as the Kent Street Quarry. Operating from the 1830s to the early 1860s it provided sandstone for many of the notable buildings from the era that survive today, including the Sydney Observatory and Garrison Church. Part of the quarry can be seen behind the tennis courts beside the Agar Steps.

The north end of Kent Street is lined with a rich variety of 19th century terrace houses. Located at numbers 37-47, Alfreds Terrace is a notable original example of domestic Georgian style architecture. Built in 1865 the exposed sandstone facade features simple decorative elements such as 12 pane windows, stone cornices above the doorways and a projecting roof parapet.

On the corner of Kent and Argyle Streets is the former Millers Point Post Office. Constructed in 1891, it is a unique example of the Federation Free Classical style with some interesting stylistic details. The brickwork is formed using a mix of Flemish bond and stretcher bond methods. Multi-panel sash windows flank the first storey arched entrance and an oculus form on the second, while the roof is decorated with a convoluted parapet with a rendered coping.

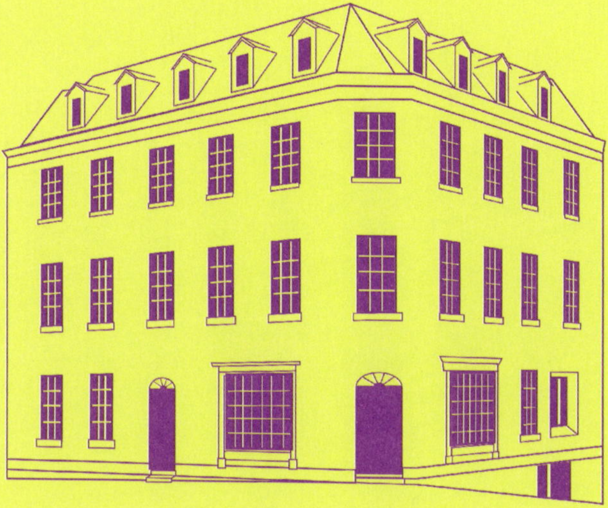

12 19 Kent St / c1836 / Michael Lehane

LORD NELSON HOTEL

Reputed to be Sydney's oldest continuously licenced pub, the Lord Nelson Hotel began trading in 1842, the same year in which the city was officially incorporated. The building was constructed around 1836 by William Wells who initially used it as his residence. Wells occupied the hotel on and off until 1870 when the premises was taken over by John Henwood and Alfred C Wells, possibly a relative. Although various changes have been made to the interiors over the years, during the 1990s the exterior was restored in a manner that reflects the original appearance of the building.

Built of sandstone quarried from nearby Observatory Hill the hotel represents the Old Colonial Regency style that was popular in Australia during the early 19th century. Rectangular sash windows punctuate the facades with large, fixed, timber framed glazing on either side of the corner entrance. The Argyle Street and corner entrance are both arched with decorative fanlights. Unusually, for a large building in this style, rendering of the stonework is restricted to a painted ground level band running along the Argyle Street facade and continuing down the sloping Kent Street side, articulated by a broad string course.

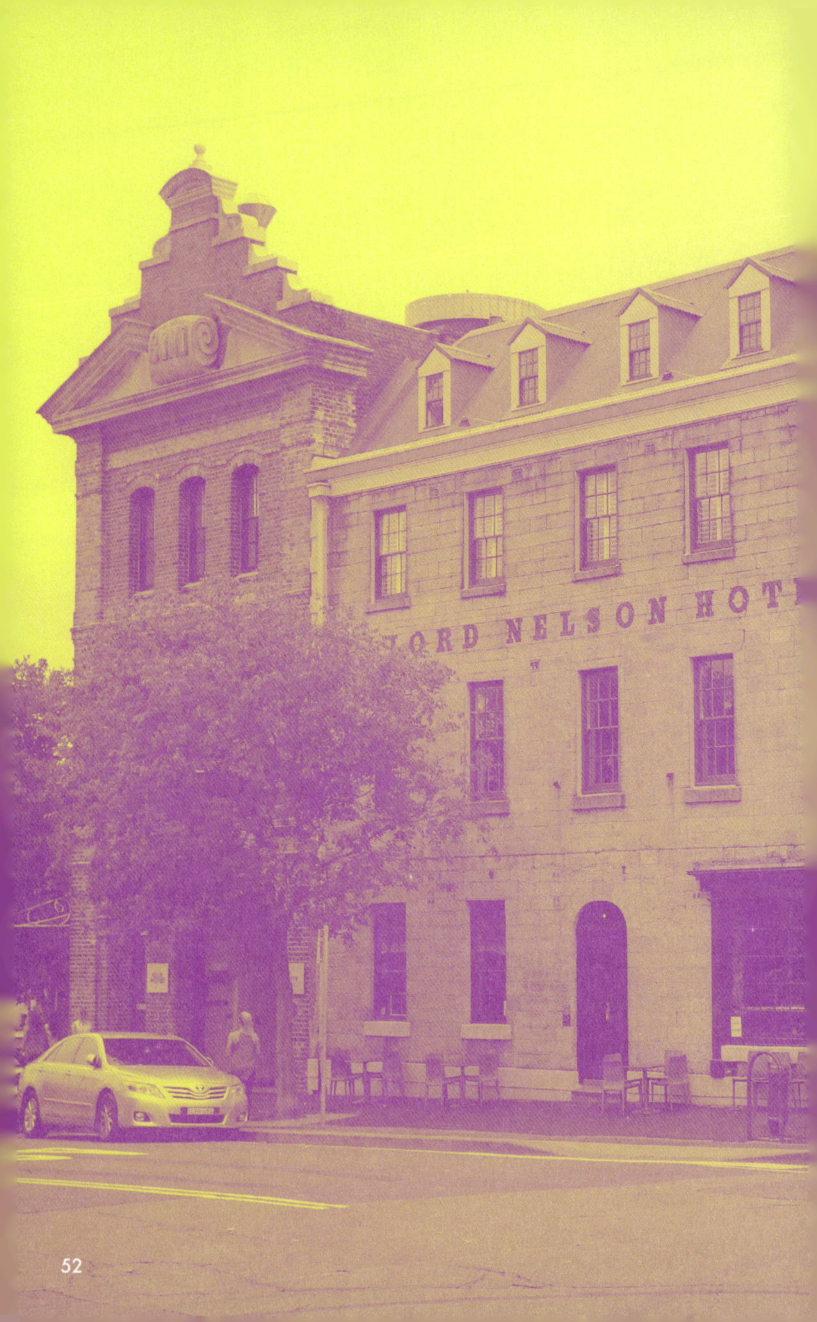
ORD NELSON HOT

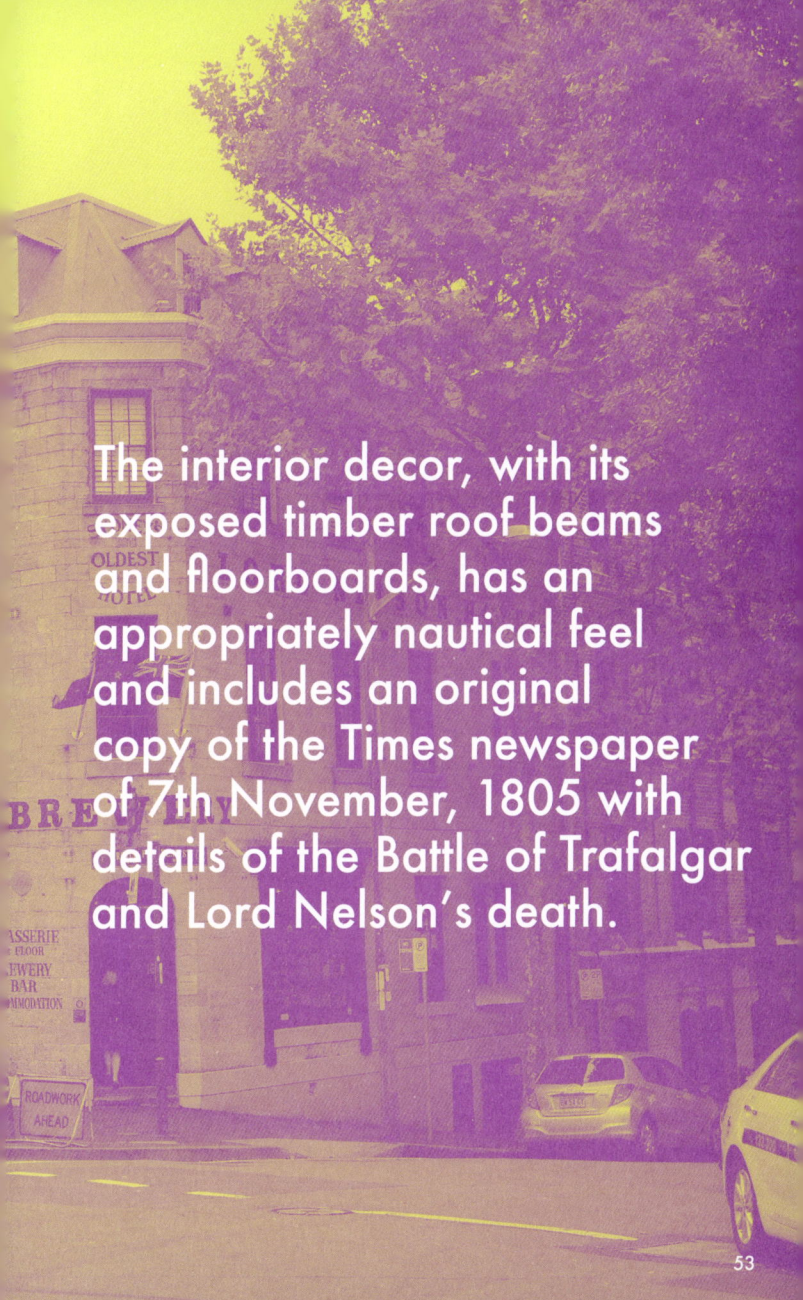

The interior decor, with its exposed timber roof beams and floorboards, has an appropriately nautical feel and includes an original copy of the Times newspaper of 7th November, 1805 with details of the Battle of Trafalgar and Lord Nelson's death.

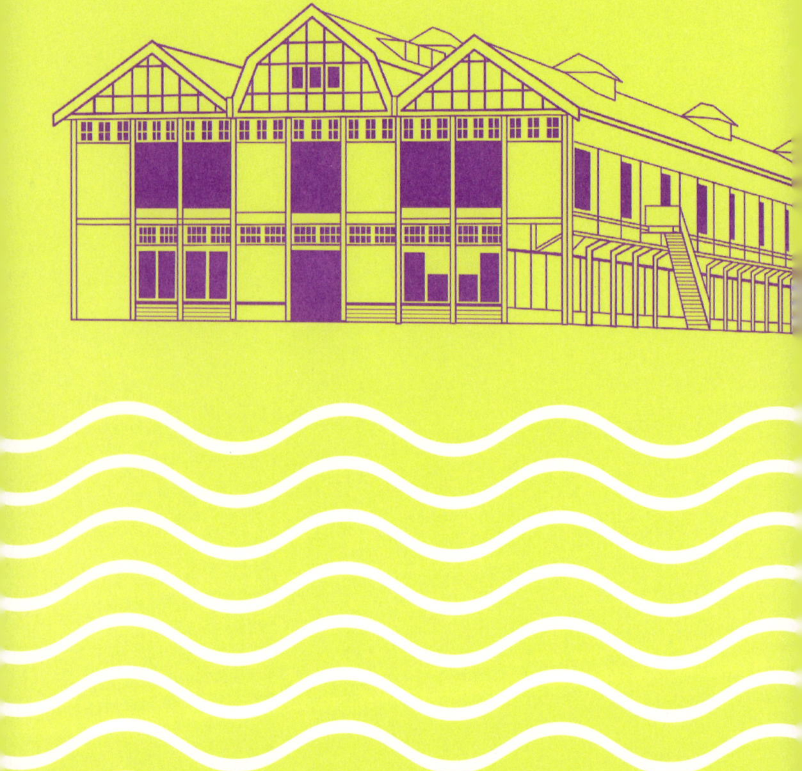

13 Hickson Rd / 1912-21

WALSH BAY WHARVES

Built as part of the early 20th century reconstruction of the Millers Point area, the Walsh Bay Wharves were a vital component of Sydney's maritime infrastructure until the 1970s. The complex is comprised of a long shore wharf (Pier 1), four finger wharves (Piers 2-9) and a series of shore sheds along Hickson Road.

The wharves are constructed of timber piles of up to 40 metres driven into the bedrock below. Timber planks originally formed the decking, later being replaced with concrete. The wharf sheds are simply built using the post and beam method with steel trusses and the walls and roofs are clad mainly in galvanised iron. The shore sheds are constructed in a similar manner with the addition of brick facades facing Hickson Road. The two-storey facades of the three separate structures reflect the popular Federation Free Style of the time with multiple decorative banding, expressed brick pilasters and geometric parapet forms. The shed facade fronting piers eight and nine is particularly ornate with two large arched windows framed by pointed stone voussoirs. Various industrial artefacts can be seen throughout the complex including hoists, floor hatches, hydraulic pumps and wool bale elevators.

From 1982, after years of disuse, the wharves were gradually redeveloped into an entertainment and cultural precinct and are now home to restaurants, apartments and the Sydney Theatre Company.

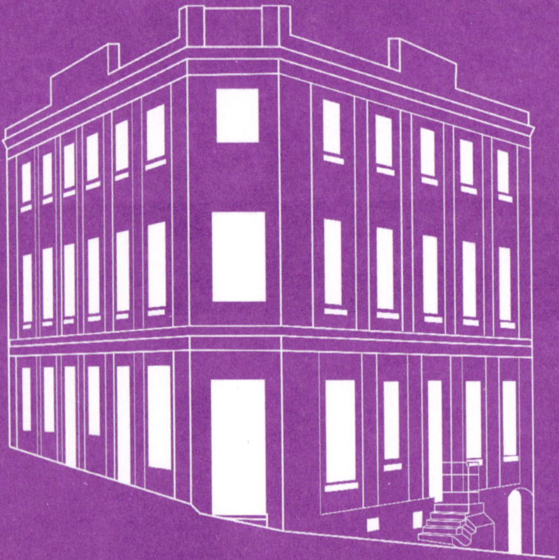

14 81 Lower Fort St / 1843

HERO OF WATERLOO HOTEL

Sharing both a corner location and reference in its name to a British military legend, the Hero of Waterloo can also claim, along with the Lord Nelson Hotel, to be one of Sydney's oldest drinking establishments. The building was constructed in 1844 by Scottish stonemason George Paton, who also worked on the Garrison Church. A year later the pub was licenced and was soon busy serving a clientele of seafarers and colonial troops.

The three-storey structure is built from rough faced sandstone with a broad rendered string course running between the first and second levels. Georgian style rectangular sash windows punctuate the facade and the hipped roof is decorated with simple parapets. The interior has witnessed few dramatic changes over the years apart from the expansion of the main bar in 1928 when a partition wall was removed.

⭐ OF NOTE

Parbury Ruins (Corner Windmill & Pottinger Streets)

The remains of an early 19th century stone cottage can be seen at this site. Discovered during excavation work for a new apartment complex in 2000, and subsequently preserved in the basement level, the dwelling was built by Hugh Noble sometime around 1820. It was sold to Thomas Street in 1831 who added a basement and kitchen in 1835. By the 1860s the cottage had been abandoned and partly demolished. Please note that although access is by appointment only, the site can be illuminated and viewed through the glass.

The pub's cellar, which can be visited, features a secret tunnel that leads to the harbour. Legend has it that during the 19th century it was used for various nefarious activities including rum smuggling and the shanghaiing of drunken patrons to crew undermanned ships. True or not these stories add to the historical texture of this long standing establishment.

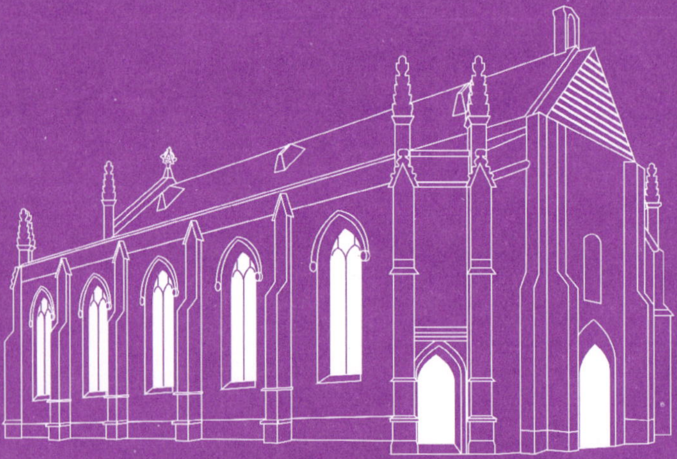

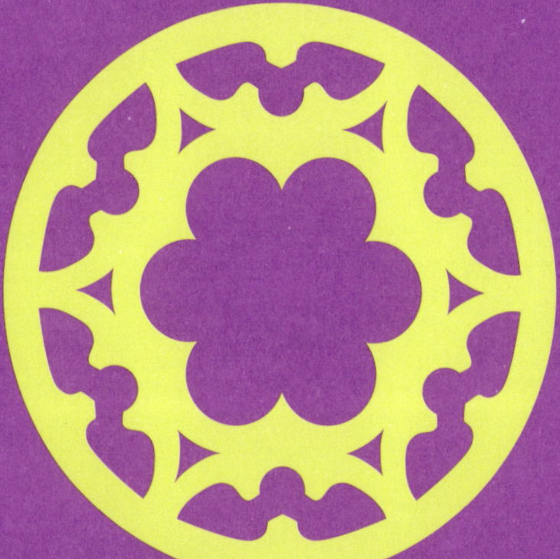

15 60 Lower Fort St / 1844 / Henry Ginn

THE GARRISON CHURCH

By the late 1830s increasing maritime activities around Millers Point were drawing a larger number of Anglican parishioners to the area than the sole church (St Philip's, established 1797) could cope with. A community meeting was convened in December 1839 resulting in a petition being sent to Governor Sir George Gipps for the establishment of a new parish. Permission was granted in January 1840 and the foundation stone for the new church was laid on the 23rd of June by Bishop William Broughton. Although construction began rapidly the depression of the 1840s soon slowed things down and by 1844 Bishop Broughton decided to allow Rev. John Couch Grylls to commence services in the partially built church. In 1855 architect Edmund Blacket was commissioned to complete the building and by 1878 the church appeared as it does to this day.

Gothic in style, the church is constructed of locally quarried sandstone with a slate roof. Externally the wide central nave is flanked on the north and south elevations by buttress forms and stone tracery windows, five to each side. The windows are decorated with label moulds and foliage bosses whilst the corner buttresses are topped by elaborate carved stone pinnacles. Internally two stone arcades, formed by five arches, run the length of the nave.

During its early years the church was regularly attended by garrison troops stationed at the nearby Dawes Point Battery, an association with the military that continued well into the 20th century.

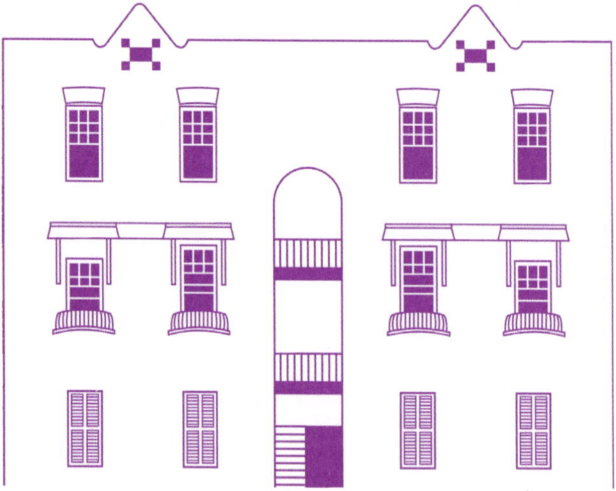

16 30-42 Lower Fort St / 1910 / Walter Vernon

WORKERS FLATS

In 1900, on the pretext of eradicating the recent outbreak of bubonic plague from the area, the NSW Government took control of and demolished hundreds of dwellings it considered slums. Over the next few years a process of reconstruction was initiated and a new supply of worker housing was built throughout Millers Point and The Rocks.

Walter Liberty Vernon migrated to Australia from England in 1883 and by 1890 was appointed government architect, working in the NSW Department of Public Works. Tasked with designing workers flats on Lower Fort Street, he drew up a plan for five semi-detached blocks of three storeys each.

Since arriving in Sydney, Vernon had become well known for his fondness for the prevailing Federation architectural styles, and the new flats gave him the opportunity to express this affinity. Designed in what is now referred to as the Federation Free Style, each block is constructed in red brick with darker decorative elements around the sash windows. A brick string course delineates the ground and first floors and alternating triangular and arched gable parapets crown each block. Curiously, block 40-42 has its upper facade rendered with more decorative features including expressed brickwork arches above the second floor windows and entablatures with dentils above those on the third floor. An interesting design feature between each block is the use of projecting, angled window bays for the upper floors, enabling maximum light to enter the rooms.

Retiring from his government post in 1911, Walter Vernon died in 1914, leaving behind a rich legacy of Federation inspired architecture throughout Sydney and New South Wales.

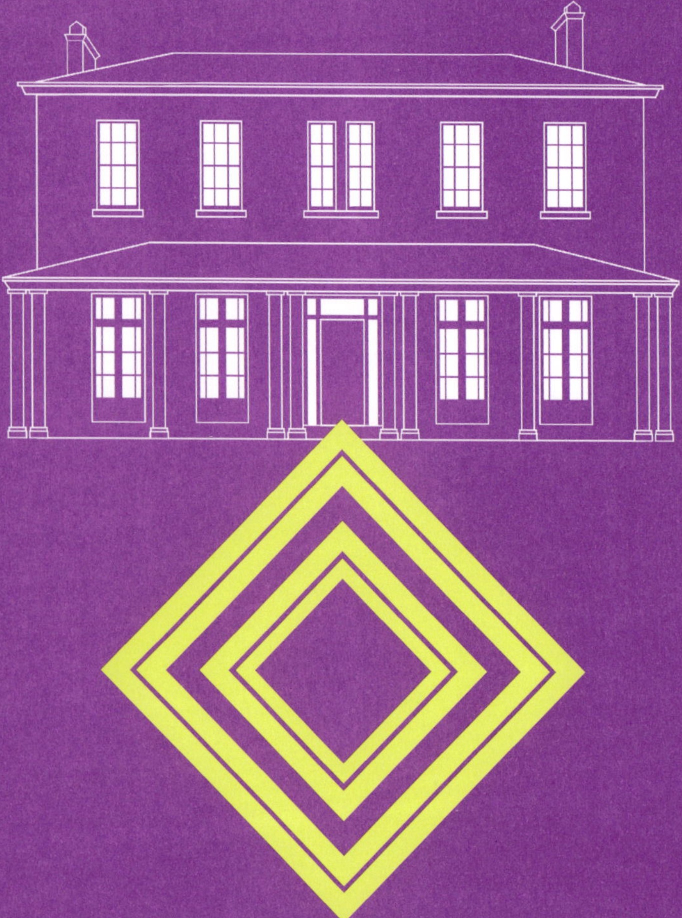

17 43 Lower Fort St / 1825

CLYDEBANK

In 1825 Robert Crawford, Principal Clerk to the Colonial Secretary, wrote to his father in Scotland informing him that "I am just finishing a house near Dawes Battery – I call it Clyde Bank, it looks into Cockle Bay and is ten minutes' walk from the office." Crawford had arrived in Sydney in 1821 and was granted the land on which he built his residence in 1823.

The two-storey rendered brick house is a highly original domestic example of Old Colonial Regency architecture. Windows and doors are symmetrically arranged with four French doors on the first level (exhibiting offset glazing beads typical of the Regency style) and five bays of sash windows on the second. The central window is an unusual feature being divided into two narrow panels by a stone pier. The slate verandah roof is supported by ten Doric columns and elegantly matches the hipped villa roof above. Both the garage and structure linking it to the main building are relatively recent additions designed in appropriate period styles.

Unfortunately Robert Crawford wasn't able to enjoy his new home for long, being forced to sell it in 1828 due to financial difficulties.

✪ OF NOTE

Iron Urinal

Originally located on Observatory Hill, the cast iron 'pissoir' on George Street (under the Sydney Harbour Bridge) was fabricated around 1880 as part the council's program to provide public toilets throughout the city. Featuring highly ornate panels decorated in the Italianate style, the facility was designed by an English firm founded by George Jennings, a sanitary engineer who invented the first public flush toilets.

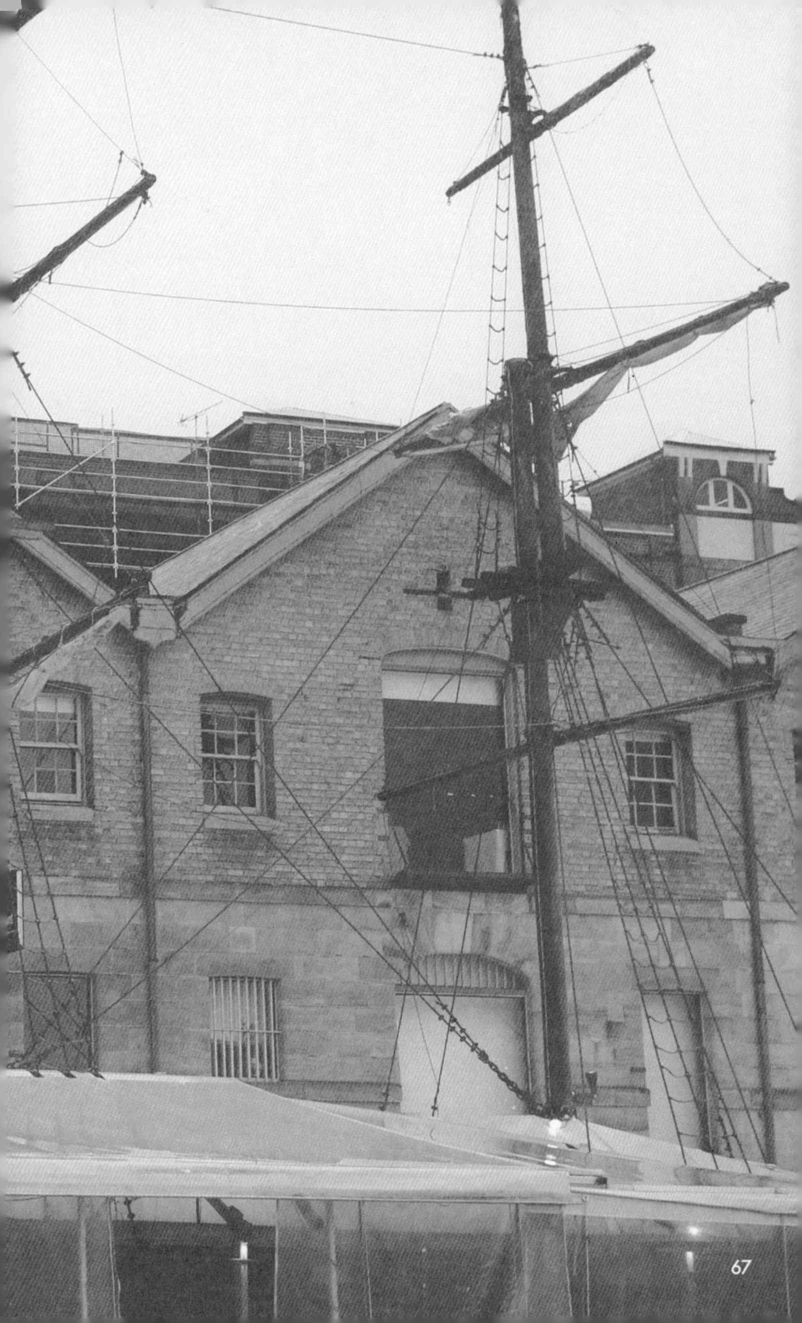

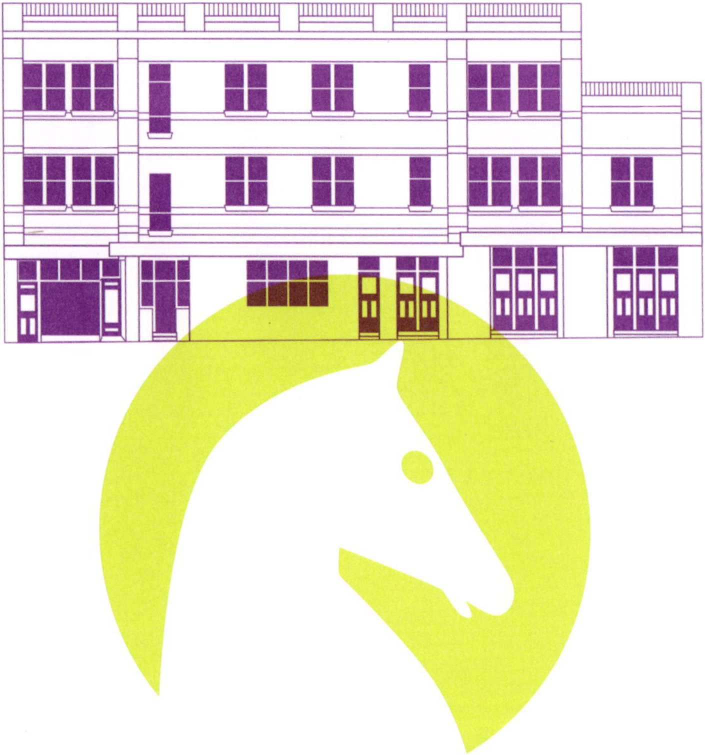

18 25-27 George St Nth / 1914

THE MERCANTILE HOTEL

Trading continuously since 1915, the Mercantile Hotel was built as part of brewer Tooth & Co.'s expansion throughout the early 20th century. In 1835 John Tooth started a brewery in Sydney with his brother-in-law John Newnham. Business was good and by the late 19th century the Tooth family had interests in a variety of fields including real estate and banking. The dawn of the 20th century saw Tooth & Co as the dominant brewer in NSW and the company continued to expand via the acquisition of rival breweries and malt producers. Building or buying hotels was another effective way of cornering the beer market due to the tied house system, meaning the licensee was obligated to market the brewer's products exclusively. This practice was outlawed in 1974.

Constructed on the site previously occupied by the Mercantile Rowing Club Hotel (1878) the building is considered a subdued example of the Federation Free Style. The red brick facade, punctuated by single pane rectangular sash windows, is decorated with rendered cream bands. A simple corniche form sits below the roof, which features ornate iron balustrades. The most ostentatious feature of the exterior is the glazed green tiled section of wall at street level which, stylistically, is more closely associated with Art Nouveau than Federation architecture.

One of Australia's oldest companies, Tooth & Co. witnessed many changes of fortune over subsequent decades, ceasing to function as an independent entity in 1983 after the first of many corporate takeovers by various business concerns.

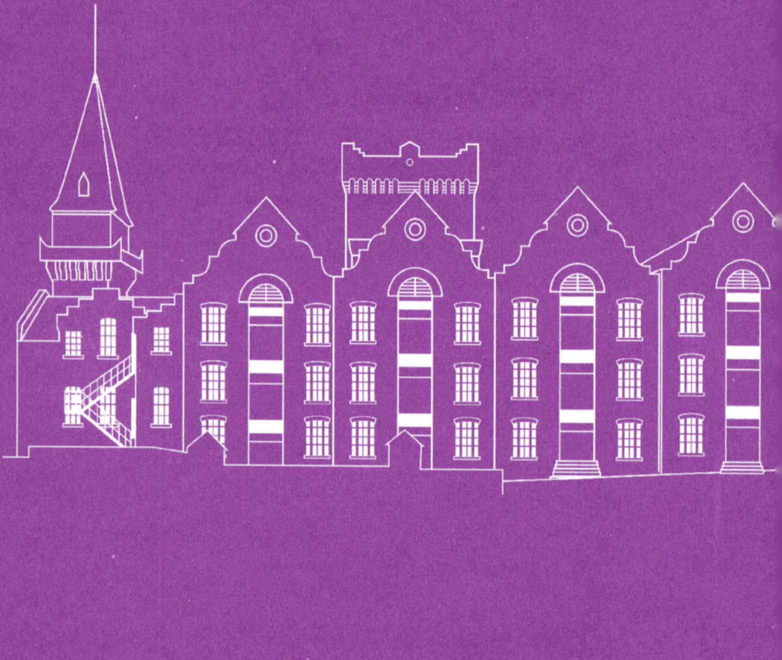

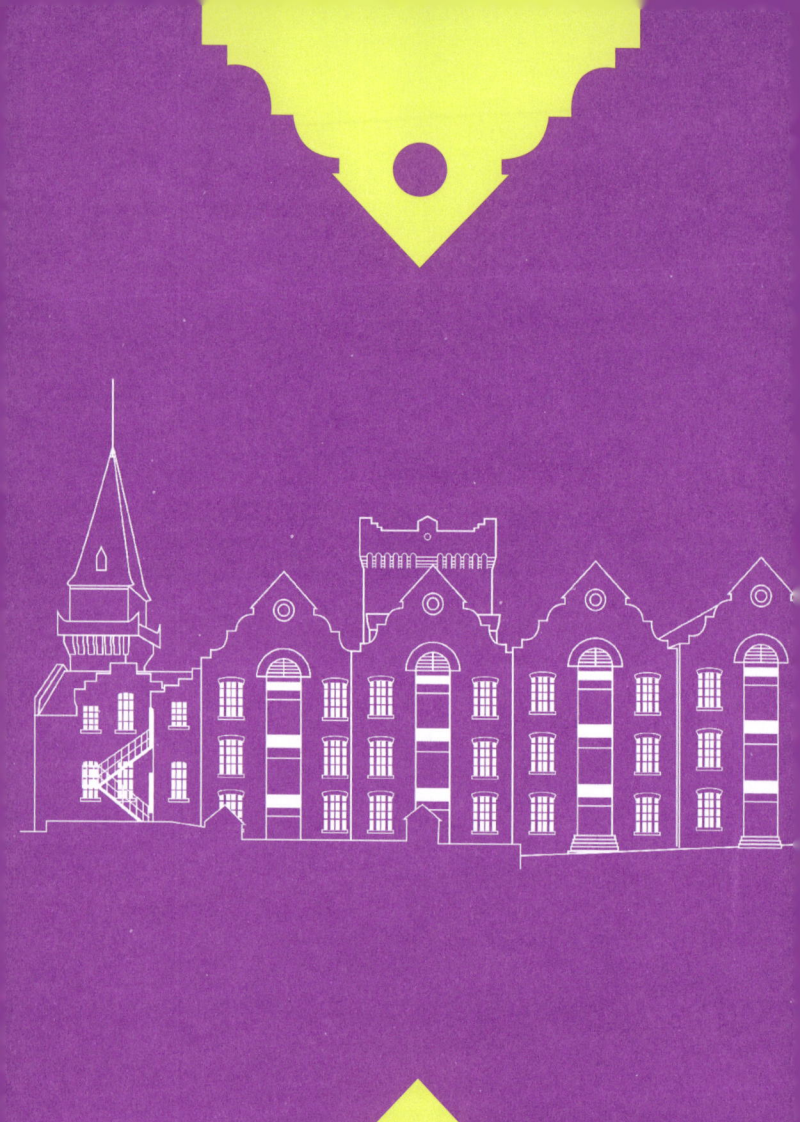

19 1-5 Hickson Rd / 1884 / William Wardell

AUSTRALASIAN STEAM NAVIGATION COMPANY

The Hunter River Steam Navigation Company was founded in 1839, reforming in 1851 as the Australasian Steam Navigation Company. Acquiring prominent waterfront land in 1876 the company proceeded to construct the new premises that would serve as its main offices and warehouse.

The building was designed by William Wardell, an architect who had moved to Sydney in 1878 having primarily worked in Melbourne since his arrival from England in 1858. His previous works included Victoria's Government House (1876) and St Mary's Cathedral in Sydney, one of the largest ecclesiastical buildings in Australia. With the ASN project Wardell introduced a very early example of Federation Anglo-Dutch architecture to the city. The first floor stone base gives way to red-brown brick work with red brick decorative features in the form of window head arches and horizontal banding.

The warehouse facades each have a central loading bay topped by a brickwork arch. Rising five floors they are crowned by stone capped Dutch gables featuring an oculus, below which can be seen the old hoist pulleys. The facades facing Hickson Road are staggered and appear to descend below the rising street. The large fortress-like structure sitting atop the warehouses is a water tower that was added in 1894. The adjoining office is designed in a similar manner to the warehouse facades with the addition of a prominent central clock tower.

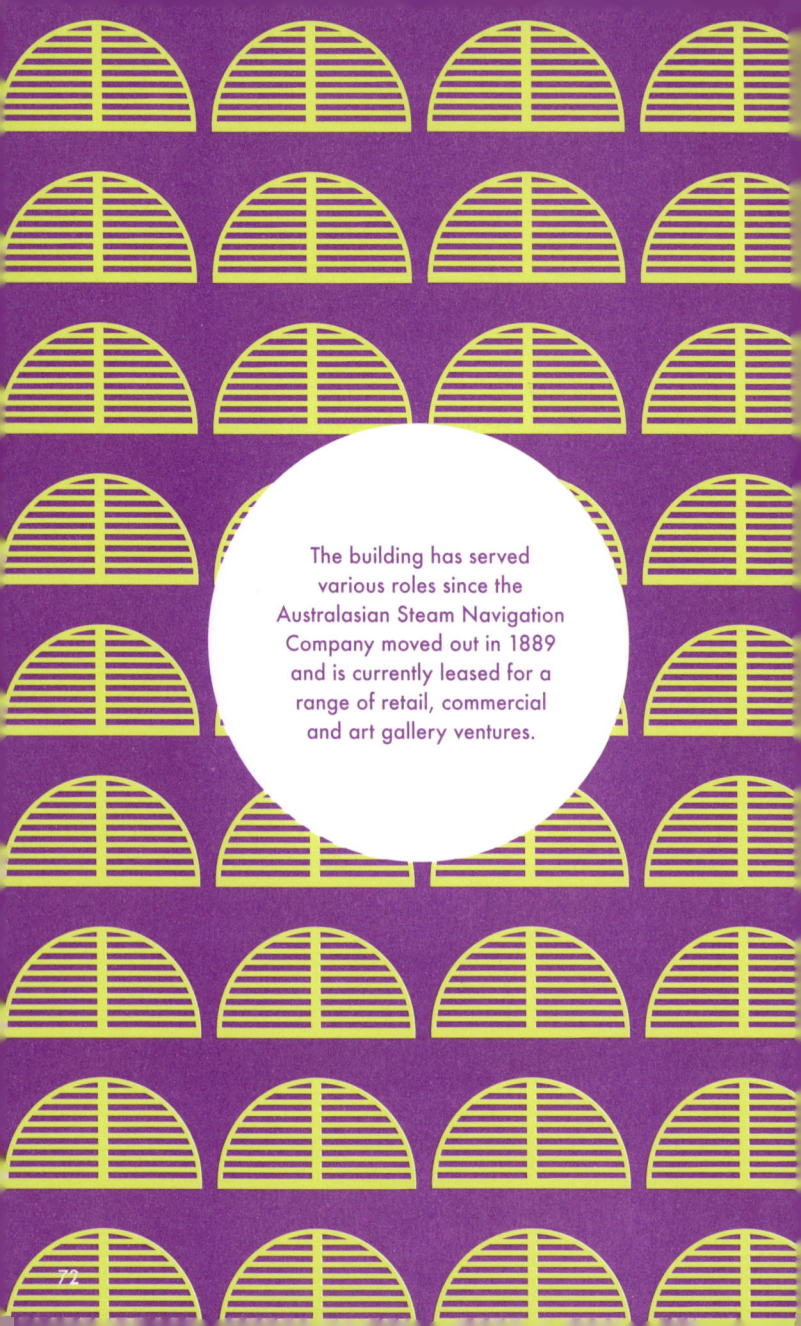

The building has served various roles since the Australasian Steam Navigation Company moved out in 1889 and is currently leased for a range of retail, commercial and art gallery ventures.

73

✪ OF NOTE

Campbell's Stores / 1851-61 / 7-27 Circular Quay West

Comprised of 11 bays of three storeys each, Campbell's Stores are a rare surviving example of mid-19th century Georgian warehouse architecture on Sydney's foreshore. Robert Campbell was a Scottish merchant who arrived in Australia in 1798, and built up a thriving business over the following decades. Initially two storeys high, a third brick level was added to each bay around 1882.

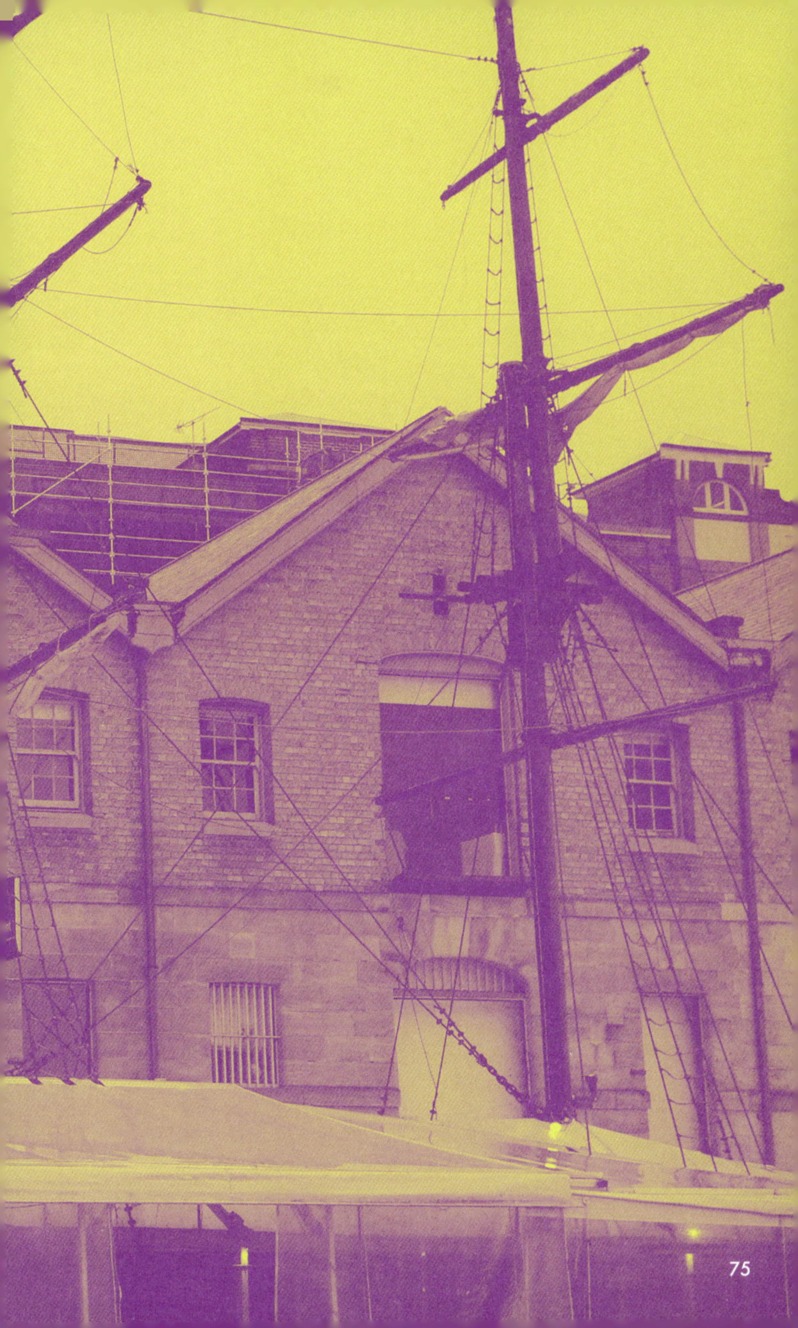

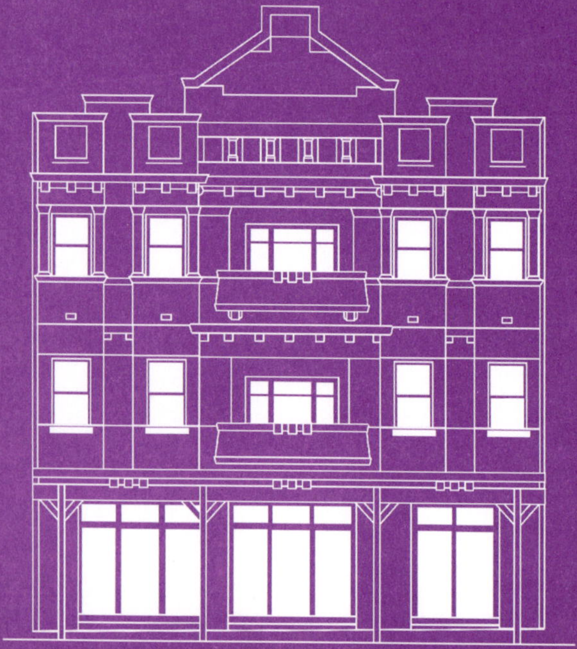

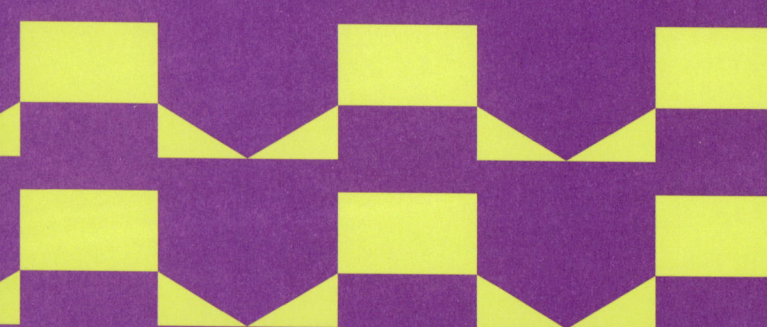

20 69 George St / 1908 / Halligan & Wilton

OBSERVER HOTEL

Commissioned by brewer Tooth & Co., the Observer Hotel is another example of a Federation Free Style design incorporating Art Nouveau elements. Built on what was originally part of the old hospital's medicinal plant gardens (1788-1816), the hotel replaced an earlier licenced premises called the Observer Tavern (1848). An uncommon name for a public house, it is thought to have been inspired by the construction of the Sydney Observatory in the same year.

The three-storey facade is red brick highlighted with mustard yellow cement rendering. Central recessed balconies on the second and third storeys are flanked on either side by two bays of sash windows. An unbroken cornice with dentil moulding crowns the top floor and marks the transition of the expressed bays into parapet elements. The moulded floral motifs within each element, along with the Observer Hotel script on the pediment, reflect the emerging Art Nouveau decorative style that was increasingly being used in early 20th century Australian hotel architecture.

OBSERVER HOTEL

Although the interior has been altered significantly over the years, the hotel's exterior remains original and is a significant surviving example of The Rocks post-plague rebuilding effort.

FRANCIS GREENWAY

(1777-1837)

Partly responsible for Sydney's earliest surviving residential structure (supervising the design and construction of Cadmans Cottage in 1816), Francis Howard Greenway came to Australia as a convict in February 1814.

He was born in Gloucestershire, near Bristol, and went on to become an architect of some merit before bankruptcy led him to commit the crime of forgery. Sentenced to death, Greenway was lucky to have his sentence later commuted to 14 years transportation to the colony of New South Wales.

Arriving in Sydney with architectural portfolio and letters of recommendation in hand, Greenway was soon granted permission to seek private work to support himself and his family who had arrived in March 1814.

NSW Governor Lachlan Macquarie was keen to improve the quality of civic buildings in the colony and, impressed by Greenway's credentials, commissioned him to design a variety of structures from 1816 onwards.

Greenway's first project, the lighthouse at the entrance to Port Jackson, so impressed the Governor that he was emancipated and given the role of Acting Civil Architect. Over the next few years Greenway was responsible for the design of numerous prominent buildings including Hyde Park Barracks (1819), St James Church (1824) and Old Government House.

He also designed the obelisk that sits in Macquarie Park in central Sydney. Employed as a point from which to record distances to various locations in NSW, it shares the park with an anchor from the 'Sirius', a ship from the First Fleet.

Greenway fell out of favour with Macquarie over what the Governor took to be increasingly exorbitant fees and, in 1822, the architect was dismissed from his post by incoming Governor Thomas Brisbane. Although he continued in private practice Greenway never attained his previous success and remained bitter over his treatment to the end. He died of typhoid on his farm near Newcastle in 1837.

Many of his buildings have survived to the present day and are celebrated as significant and valued examples of Sydney's early built heritage. This led, rather ironically for a convicted forger, to his portrait being used on Australia's first ten dollar note.

THE ROCKS TIMELINE
1788-1826

Pre-1788 Occupied for thousands of years by indigenous tribes, the area now known as The Rocks was most recently home to the Gadigal or Eora people.

1788 The First Fleet arrives in Sydney Cove on January 26 under the command of Captain Arthur Phillip, the first Governor of NSW.

1793 The first free settlers arrive.

1808 Governor William Bligh is deposed by members of the NSW Corps. The event becomes known as the Rum Rebellion.

1810 Governor Lachlan Macquarie initiates extensive town planning and building reforms.

1816 Convict architect Francis Greenway supervises the construction of Cadmans Cottage. In the same year he also draws up plans for Sydney's first lighthouse, completed in 1818.

1823 Population of The Rocks area is estimated to be around 1200, the majority convicts and their children.

1826 One of the first substantial buildings is erected on Argyle Street. Constructed of stone, it serves as Sydney's first Customs House.

THE ROCKS TIMELINE
1840–1923

1840 The end of convict transportation to NSW.

1843 Construction of the Argyle Cut commences.

1850s Land subdivision and housing developments, along with paving and drainage works, begin to transform The Rocks and Millers Point into a more diversely populated neighbourhood.

1870 Last British troops depart the colony.

1888 Sydney celebrates its centenary.

1900 Bubonic plague breaks out in Millers Point, eventually resulting in the demolition of hundreds of dwellings throughout the area.

1901 Federation of the six colonies, establishing the nation of Australia.

1923 Construction of the Sydney Harbour Bridge begins, resulting in the realignment of streets and demolition of various structures in Millers Point and The Rocks.

GLOSSARY

Boss: A decorative protrusion of stone or wood

Buttress: A structure of masonry or brick used to provide lateral support to a wall

Campanile: Italian term for bell tower

Classical Order: A principal component of classical architecture comprising base, shaft, capital and entablature

Colonial Georgian/Regency: An Australian take on similar English styles emphasising symmetry and proportion. Georgian was generally sparsely decorated as opposed to the Regency style which incorporated subtle classical elements and motifs. Popular from settlement to the mid-19th century.

Coping: The capping or covering of a wall

Corinthian: One of the five classical orders, characterised by acanthus leaves decorating the capitals

Cornice: A continuous horizontal moulding crowning a building or aperture

Dentil Moulding: A small block used in repetition as a decorative feature on a cornice

Entablature: The structure above the capital comprising architrave, frieze and cornice

Facade: An exterior side of a building, often referring to the front

Federation Style: Encompassing various revival styles popular in England around 1890-1915 (including Queen Anne and Edwardian) Federation architecture utilised, amongst other elements, extensive brickwork and decorative roof features.

Freestone: A soft stone used in masonry for carving, moulding and tracery (eg sandstone)

Frieze: The central component of the entablature, often decorated with a relief design

Gable: The triangular part of a wall between the sloping faces of a pitched roof

Gallery: A platform raised above a church floor

Ionic: One of the five classical orders, characterised by a scroll-like ornament decorating the capital and often fluted shaft

Label Mould: A projecting element over an opening

Loggia: A covered exterior gallery enclosed on one side by arcades or colonnades.

Mansard: French style four-sided roof

Nave: The main body of a church building

Palladian: A style inspired by the 16th century architect Andrea Palladio. Primarily based on principles of symmetry, perspective and values of the formal classical temple architecture of Greece and Rome.

Parapet: A vertical extension of the facade wall at the edge of a roof

Pavilion: A structural emphasis placed at the end of a symmetrical building's wings

Pediment: A classical triangular shaped structure placed above the entablature of a building

Pier: An upright element or section providing structural support

Pilasters: A column feature projecting from the face of a wall (as opposed to a free standing column)

Portico: A porch extending from the main body of a building

Pulpit: The raised stand for speakers in a church

String Course: A thin horizontal band, usually of stone or brick, running along a wall to delineate floors

Quoin: Cornerstones of a wall, often rusticated.

Rustication: A masonry technique used to accentuate the joins between stone blocks. The face of each block is also often given a rough or patterned finish to further delineate each stone.

Voussoir: A wedge shaped element that forms part of an arch.

THE WALK

The Footpath Guide to
The Rocks architecture in
Sydney takes approximately
1.5 hours to complete.

CONTENTS

3	Architectural Beginnings
7	The Rise of Modernism
11	Sydney Opera House
15	AMP Building
19	Governor Phillip Tower
23	Liner House
25	Suncorp Place
27	Grosvenor Place
31	Sirius Apartments
35	Blues Point Tower
37	Gold Fields House
39	51 Pitt Street
41	Australia Square
45	Guardian Assurance Building
47	Currency House
49	Qantas House
53	Pearl Assurance Building
55	Capita Centre
57	MLC Centre
61	Reserve Bank Building
65	Law Courts Building
67	Centrepoint
69	King George Building
71	Commonwealth Bank Building
73	Town Hall House
77	St Andrews House
79	Sydney Electricity Building
81	Sydney Masonic Centre
85	About The Architects
88	Glossary
90	Timeline

N
W
E
S

ARCHITECTURAL BEGINNINGS

When Captain Arthur Phillip sailed into Botany Bay, on the east coast of Australia, in January 1788, he was unimpressed. The bay was unprotected and shallow and surrounded by poor soil and its shore was observed to be unproductive with scarce fresh water. Having led a fleet of ships halfway around the world to found a penal colony for British convicts, he decided to explore further north for a better location.

He found it just 12 kilometres up the coast. Port Jackson was an inlet discovered and named by Captain James Cook in 1770 although it was not extensively explored at the time. What Phillip found as he ventured up the inlet was, in his opinion, 'the finest harbour in the world'.

Named after the British Home Secretary Thomas Townshend (Lord Sydney), Sydney Cove was a well sheltered deep water anchorage with ample fresh water supplies. It was a perfect site for the first official British settlement on the Australian continent.

FOR THE FIRST TWO DECADES OF SYDNEY'S EXISTENCE THE COLONY WAS SO LACKING IN APPROPRIATE SKILLS AND TOOLS THAT THE MAJORITY OF BUILDINGS CONSTRUCTED WERE OF POOR QUALITY AND IN NEED OF CONSTANT MAINTENANCE.

The situation changed dramatically with the appointment of Major-General Lachlan Macquarie as Governor of New South Wales in 1810. Finding many structures throughout the settlement in a 'most ruinous state of decay', Macquarie implemented a set of building codes that dictated a minimum standard for any future construction. Teaming up with convicted forger and architect Francis Greenway, the Governor also commissioned a series of classically inspired public buildings including Hyde Park Barracks (1819) and St James Church (1824), both of which still stand today.

From the mid to late 19th century architectural trends in Sydney closely followed those adopted throughout the British Empire. Grand classical revival styles were used extensively for public and administrative buildings whilst well to do residents displayed their wealth with elaborate Victorian Italianate or sober Georgian home designs.

THE RISE OF MODERNISM

As the 20th century dawned worldwide architectural fashions continued to make their way into Sydney's built environment, particularly during the interwar years (1919-1939). Many commercial buildings adopted the sleek Art Deco and Moderne aesthetics from Europe (David Jones Building, 1938) whilst others attempted to emulate the soaring skyscraper designs of New York and Chicago (AWA Tower, 1939).

These new styles did not, however, entirely sweep away the architectural past as many administrative and commercial buildings were still being designed in what is now termed Free Classical, complete with all the traditional motifs and orders seen throughout the 19th century.

Times were rapidly changing however and the wave of International Modernism that was transforming both architectural form and theory throughout world would inevitably reach the shores of Australia.

Although the movement had its beginnings in Europe during the early 1920s it did not make a significant impact on Australian cities until after the Second World War when architects including Robin Boyd in Melbourne and Harry Seidler in Sydney introduced Modernist architecture to the nation's built environment. Seidler's commercial work in particular (Australia Square Tower, 1967; MLC Centre, 1977) had an enormous impact on Sydney's CBD from the 1960s through to the 90s.

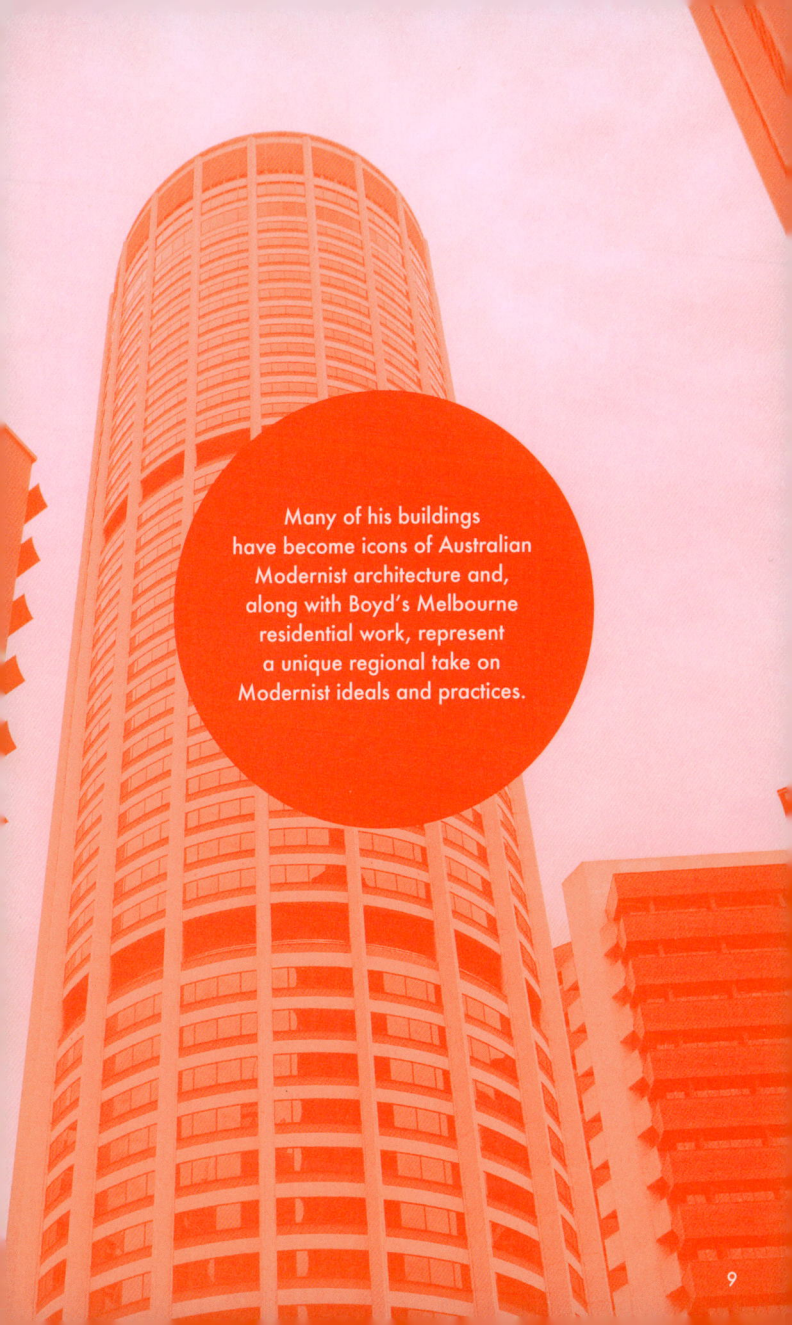

Many of his buildings have become icons of Australian Modernist architecture and, along with Boyd's Melbourne residential work, represent a unique regional take on Modernist ideals and practices.

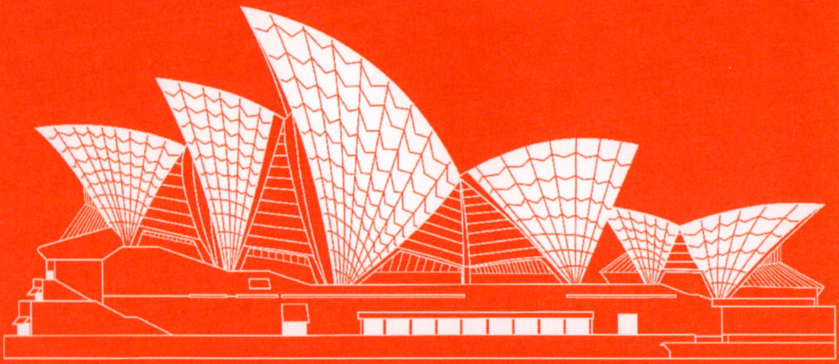

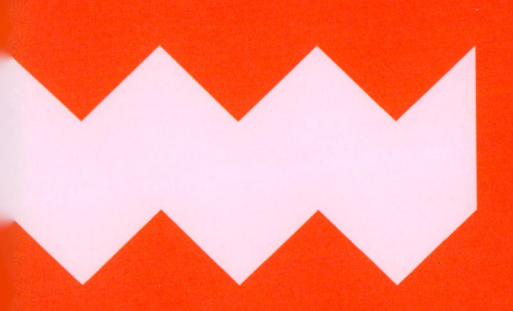

① Bennelong Point / 1973 / Jorn Utzon

SYDNEY OPERA HOUSE

Arguably the most recognised built symbol of Australia, the Sydney Opera House is one of Modernism's great sculptural achievements.

Calls for a dedicated opera house began in the late 1940s, led by the Director of the NSW State Conservatorium of Music Eugene Goossens. The main venue for large theatrical performances at the time, Sydney Town Hall, was increasingly considered inadequate and on 13 September 1955 NSW Premier Joseph Cahill launched an international design competition for a new venue. In 1957 Danish architect Jorn Utzon was announced as the winner and construction began in 1959 on Bennelong Point. The structure was built in three stages: stage one (1959-63) saw the construction of the upper podium; stage two (1963-67) the outer concrete shells; stage three (1967-73) interior design and construction.

The iconic roof shells went through numerous iterations between 1957 and 1963 before Utzon and his engineer, Ove Arup, devised a form (utilising computer aided structural analysis) that was workable from both an engineering and financial point of view.

The Sydney Opera House was formally opened on 20 October 1973, almost 20 years after it was originally conceived. The podium base is clad in locally sourced pink granite whilst the shell forms or 'sails' (actually precast concrete panels supported by ribs) are covered in 1,056,006 glossy white and matte cream tiles. The entire venue has a capacity for 5,738 people in six different spaces with the main concert hall able to hold 2,679 patrons.

Utzon died on 29 November 2008 but lived to witness the listing of the Sydney Opera House as a UNESCO World Heritage Site on 28 June 2007.

✲ OF NOTE

Tom Bass Sculpture 'Research' / 1959

Walking back towards Circular Quay will take you past
the Bennelong Apartment complex. Between the two
buildings is a stone staircase (Moore Steps, 1868) leading to
Macquarie Street. To the right of the stairs, on the apartment wall,
sits a dynamic piece of artwork by Australian sculptor Tom Bass.
It was commissioned by chemical company ICI for the curtain
wall office building constructed on this site in 1957
(Bates Smart & McCutcheon, demolished 1996).

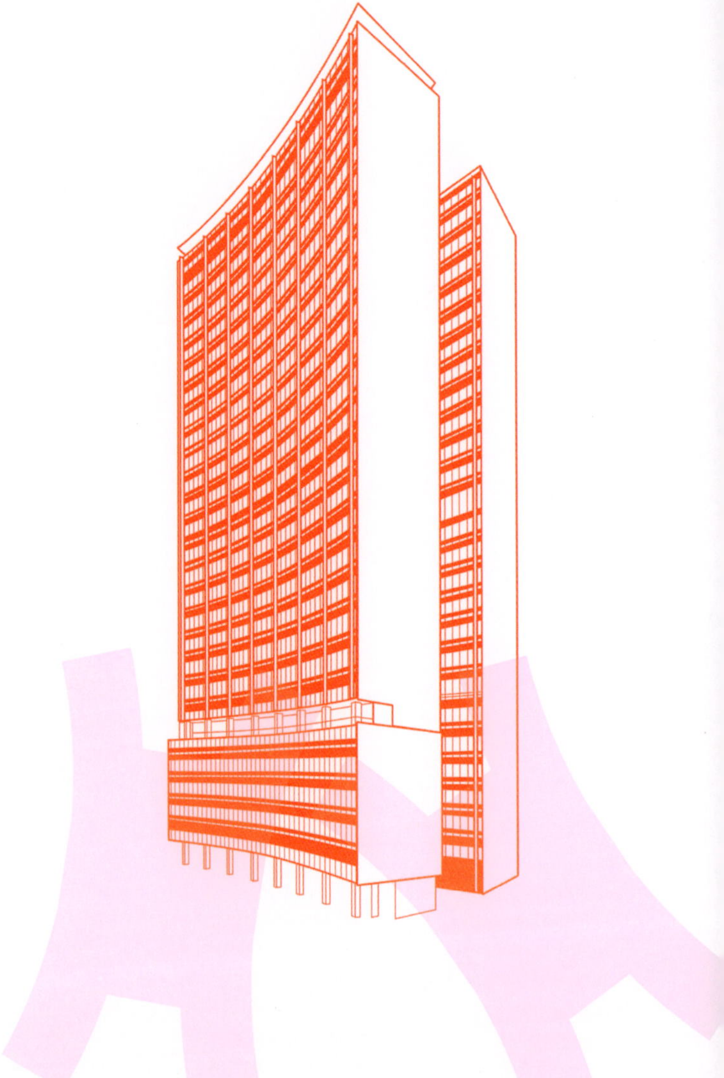

2 33 Alfred St / 1962 / Peddle Thorp and Walker

AMP BUILDING

Towering above Circular Quay the AMP building, along with nearby Gold Fields House, formed the modern 'gateway to Sydney' in the 1960s, defining the height of the city's skyscrapers until the 1980s. At 26 storeys (115 metres) the podium and tower design took the mantle of Australia's tallest building from Melbourne's ICI House (20 storeys, 1958) while using that building's precedent to break Sydney's height limit regulations (a 150 foot limit placed on city buildings in 1912).

Constructed as the new headquarters for the Australian Mutual Provident Society (a financial services company formed in 1849) the AMP Building consists of a five-storey podium supporting a 21 storey tower, sited on a large pedestrian plaza. The aluminium curtain wall is acutely defined by bronze coloured spandrels and intersecting expressed mullion elements with a further narrow band of bronze panels running across the glazing, breaking up the regular grid pattern. An increased sense of verticality is achieved in the tower design with the curtain wall sectioned into seven bays by eight narrow marble panelled columns. Extending from the base to the top, these align with the supporting columns rising from the podium structure. The overall design distinguishes itself from many other contemporary curtain wall buildings with the gentle curvature of the facade, a feature which, along with its height, caused a surprising level of controversy at the time of construction.

Although the internal office spaces have been remodelled since construction, the foyers are largely intact and still display the original marble dressing and stainless steel columns. On the Western (Young Street) facade there is a sculpture by artist Tom Bass. It depicts the goddess of Peace and Plenty flanked by the male figure of Labour on the left and a wife and child on the right. Underneath is the AMP corporation's Latin motto; "Amicus certus in re incerta" ("A certain friend in uncertain times") which, along with the three figures, could be found on many AMP buildings from the 19th century onwards.

17

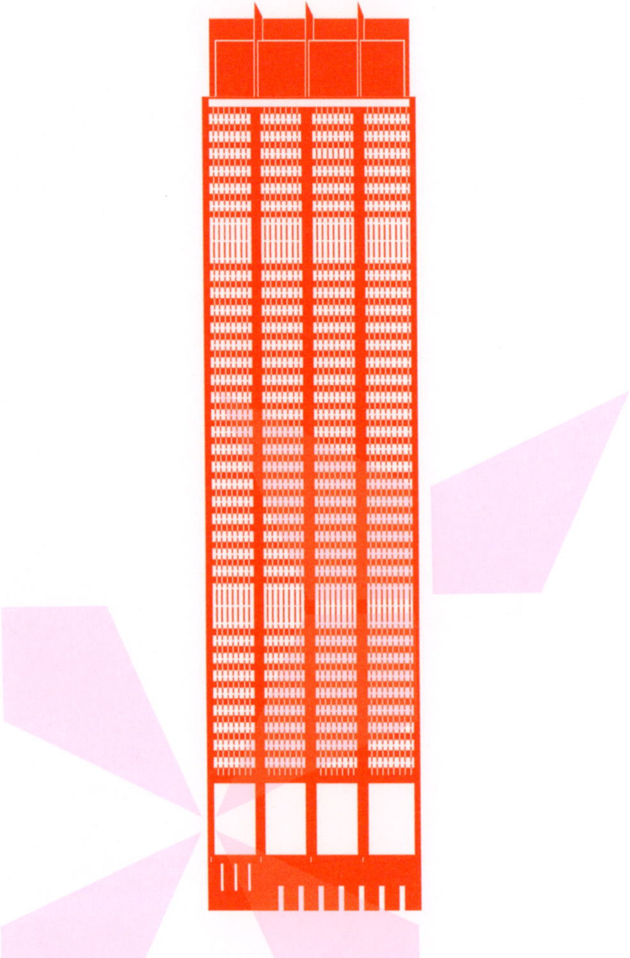

3 1 Farrer Place / 1993 / Denton Corker Marshall

GOVERNOR PHILLIP TOWER

Topping out at 227 metres Governor Phillip Tower is the third tallest building in Sydney and is located on one of Australia's most important National Heritage sites. Shortly after establishment of the new settlement of Sydney in January 1788 a building was constructed on what is now the corner of Bridge and Phillip Streets to serve as the residence for the first Governor of New South Wales, Captain Arthur Phillip. This first Government House, made of English bricks and local stone, was gradually extended and repaired by a succession of eight Governors, eventually being replaced by a new, grander structure (located near the Royal Botanic Gardens) in 1845. Demolished in 1846 the original site remained untouched until the 1980s when the present office tower was proposed for the site. Concerned heritage groups urged the NSW Government to allow archaeological exploration of the site before construction commenced and subsequent discoveries of well-preserved foundations and artefacts resulted in a re-design of the tower to preserve the findings.

Designed by Melbourne firm Denton Corker Marshall, Governor Phillip Tower forms part of a larger complex that includes Governor Macquarie Tower, First Government House Plaza and the Museum of Sydney. Sitting on a sandstone podium four storeys above street level the height of the tower is further enhanced by massive zinc-plated transfer beams that elevate the occupied floors a further six levels. The surface is clad in a flush finish of granite and glass that bestows a high quality, expensive quality upon the facades. The steel blade forms topping the roof, something of a Denton Corker Marshall design signature, have been nick-named the 'milk crate' by Sydneysiders.

The remains of First Government House (located under what is now First Government House Plaza) are partly visible through a glass pyramid in front of the entrance to the Museum of Sydney, all of which has been integrated into a modern office complex in what many consider a respectful manner.

21

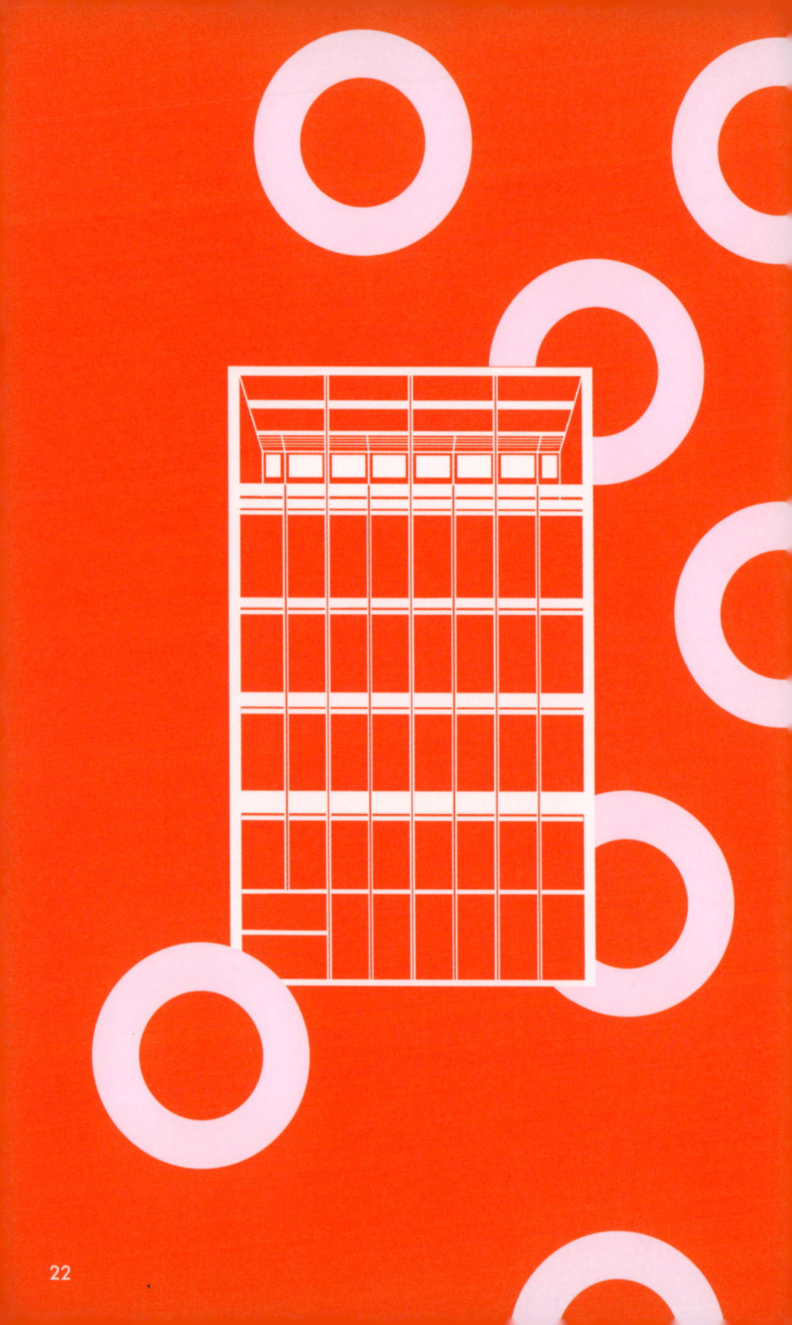

4 13-15 Bridge St / 1960 / Bunning & Madden

LINER HOUSE

Constructed as the Australian headquarters for the Wilh. Wilhelmson Agency (Norway's largest shipping company at the time) Liner House was proof that new commercial Modernist architecture could exist in harmony with existing buildings.

Instead of exploiting the site for maximum financial return the company decided to have a building designed entirely for its own use, constructed to a height that was within the scale of its immediate neighbours. Comprising a ground floor, mezzanine and four upper floors the building is set back 1.2 metres from the adjacent building facades. The curtain wall, composed of aluminium-framed windows with blue ceramic spandrel panels, is expressed horizontally by projecting sunshades with the top floor being further delineated by a framework form. In keeping with the sympathetic urban nature of the building's English Portland stone (complementing the stone used on the adjoining buildings) was used for the external flanking walls and ground floor.

Internally, Liner House still retains many of its original fittings including a spiral staircase and mural screen made of brass, copper, aluminium and stainless steel elements by Australian sculptor Douglas Annand.

In 1961 the building was awarded the prestigious Sulman Medal in recognition of its 'consistent honesty in design and good taste for this building' and 'very good manners to its neighbours'.

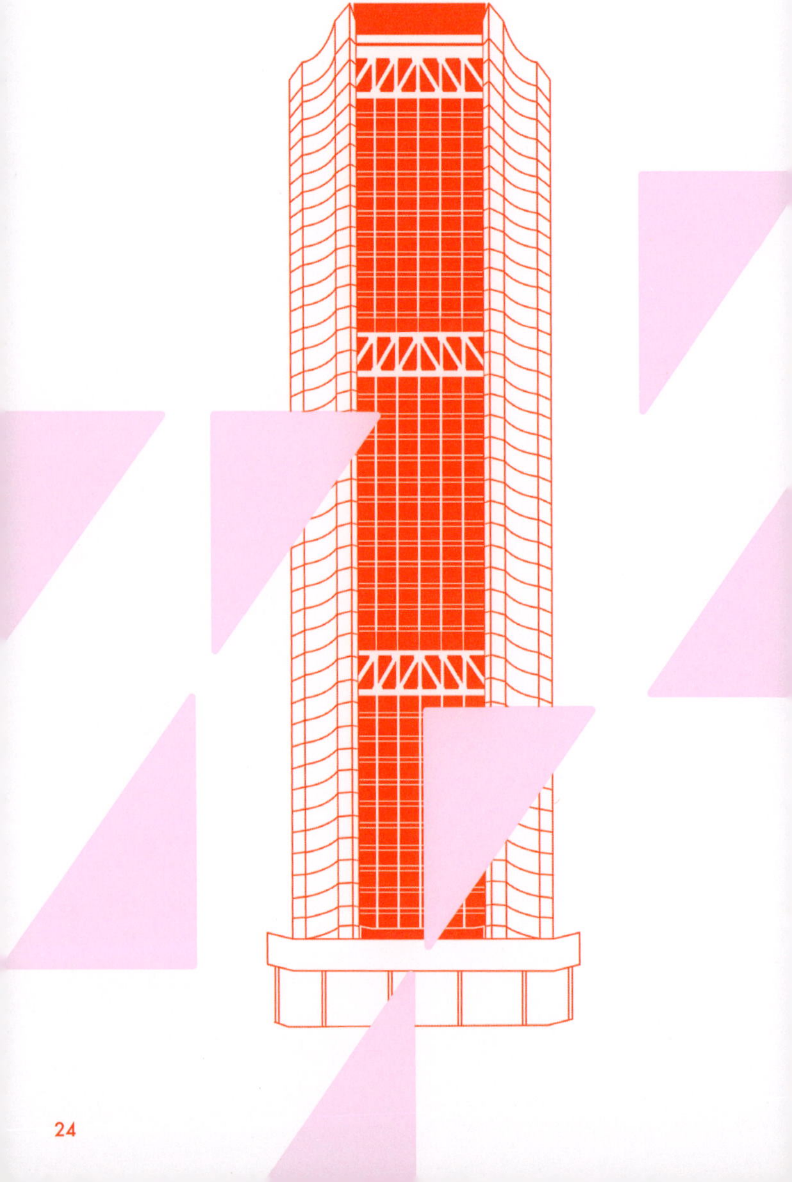

5 Cnr Grosvenor & Lang St / 1982 / Joseland & Gilling

SUNCORP PLACE

Originally designed for Qantas, the building now known as Suncorp Place was begun in 1970 but, due to union delays, wasn't completed until 1982. Realised well into the post-modern era the structure can be read as a soft fusion of late Brutalism and Hi-tech architectural styles.

Broad raw concrete columns, angled to form an elongated hexagon, flank curtain walls on each elevation. Each glazed facade is separated into three segments by horizontal concrete truss structures; functional features that express engineering form.

The building is topped by a steel cage structure that adds 18 metres to the height of Suncorp Place, making it 204 metres tall.

26

6 225 George St / 1988 / Harry Seidler

GROSVENOR PLACE

Completed in the year Australia celebrated its bicentennial, Grosvenor Place exhibits many of the regional design aspects and signature features that Harry Seidler had been developing and incorporating into his commercial work since the 1960s. The 44 floor tower is made up of two crescent-shaped halves encasing an elliptical central core, lending a unique form to the structure that can be seen as an evolution of Seidler's previous cylindrical shaped Australia Square and MLC buildings. The curved form, along with large column-free floor plates, also provides tenants with unmatched panoramic views of Sydney Harbour.

The granite-clad facade incorporates sunshades at varying angles that, along with the use of high performance thermal glazing, minimise the effects of harsh sunlight on the interiors. The sunshade elements also add textural interest to the building's surface, a practice which Siedler was fond of utilising on many of his projects, differentiating them from the usual plain Modernist grids and flush finishes.

Entry to the building is through a spectacular lobby space that expresses the curved forms of the main structure in many of its elements. Displayed on the walls of the central lift core are large artworks by American minimalist artist Frank Stella. Seidler was a big believer in large buildings as venues for the display of art and the geometry of Grosvenor Place was apparently partly inspired by Stella's work.

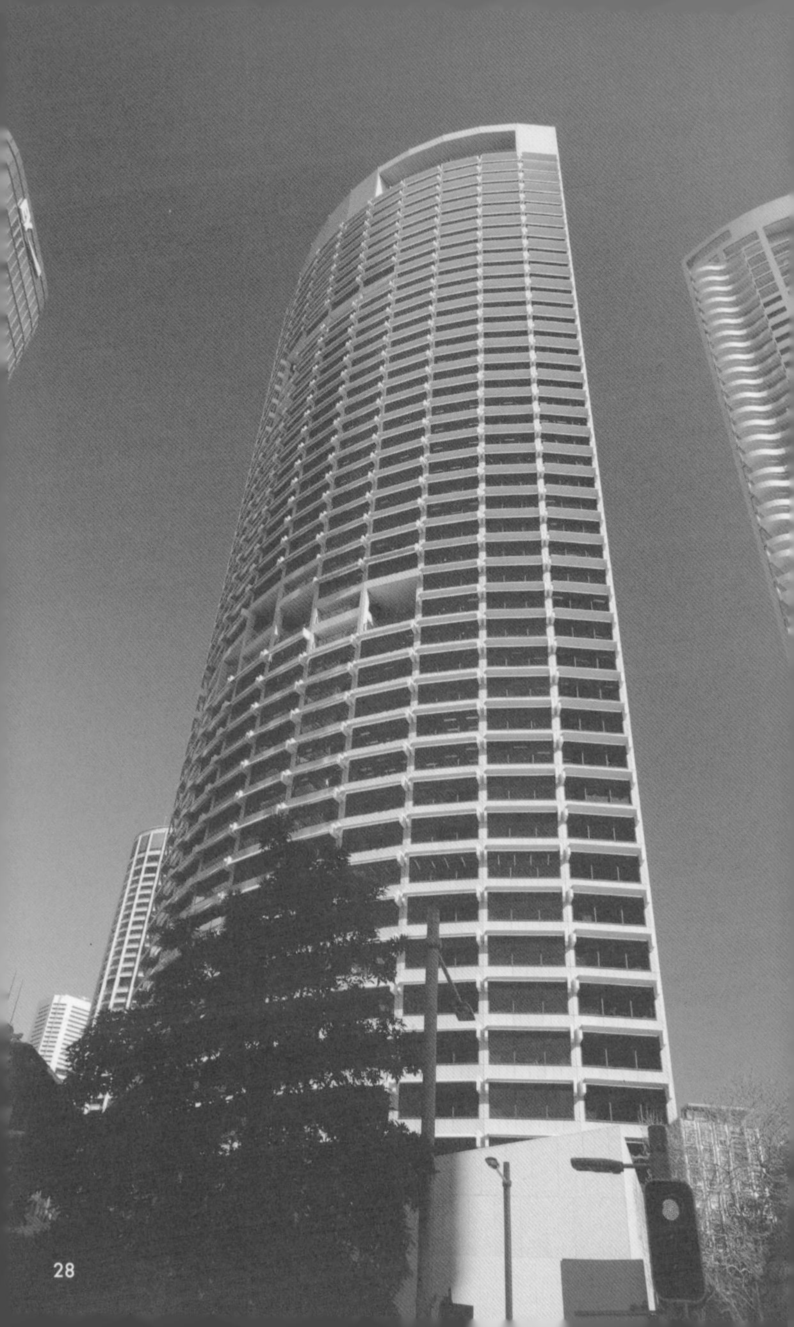

Forming a prominent transition between the historical Rocks area and the modern CBD, Grosvenor Place represents the continuing impact that Siedler's work had on Sydney's built environment throughout the late 20th century.

UNDER THREAT

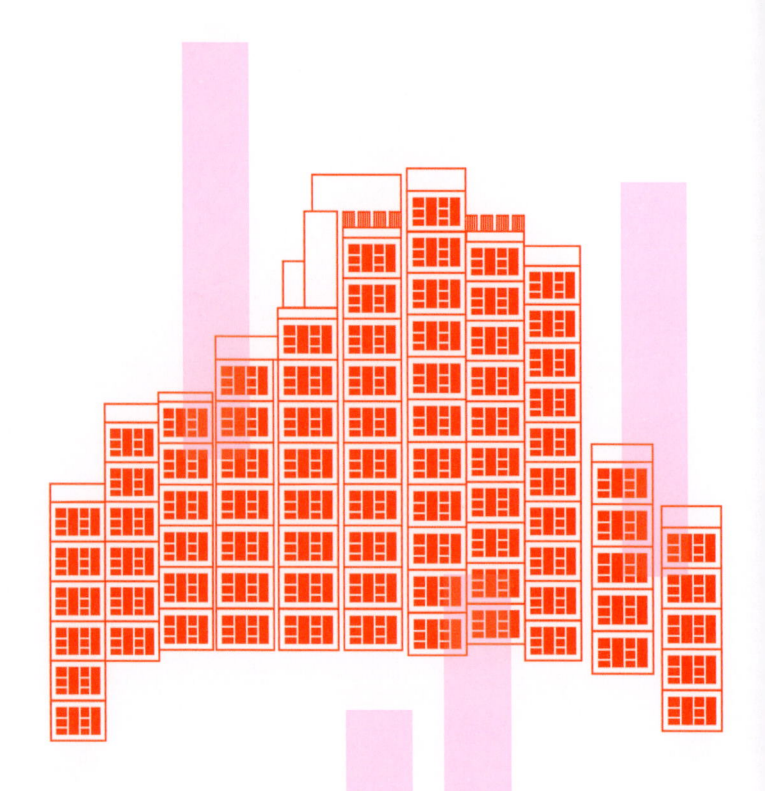

Demolition is imminent.

7 Millers Point / 1980 / Tao Gofers

SIRIUS APARTMENTS

Named after the flagship of the First Fleet that sailed into Sydney harbour in 1788, the Sirius apartment complex was built by the NSW Housing Commission to re-house public tenants of Millers Point. Throughout the 1960s and 70s heritage groups and local residents teamed up with unions to fight the NSW government's re-development proposals which would see the demolition of significant numbers of historic buildings to make way for high rise apartments and hotels.

Both the Rocks and Millers Point had long been home to a population of underprivileged and increasingly ageing residents reliant on government housing and it was the desire to enable these vulnerable people to remain in their community, whilst maintaining the working class nature of the area, that prompted the union led Green Bans of the 1970s. Although the preservation of the built heritage was really secondary to this aim the resulting planning compromises ensured that many buildings were saved.

Comprised of stacked rectangular blocks the Sirius apartment building rises and falls in an almost organic manner, as if following the topography of the landscape. The pod-like nature of the components and the raw concrete finish (the original plan to paint the building white was scrapped due to budget constraints) reflect similar projects from 1960s and 70s Japan, particularly the work of Metabolist architects such as Kiyonori Kikutake. The building was designed for both aged and family residents, providing a total of 79 one, two, three and four bedroom apartments throughout the complex.

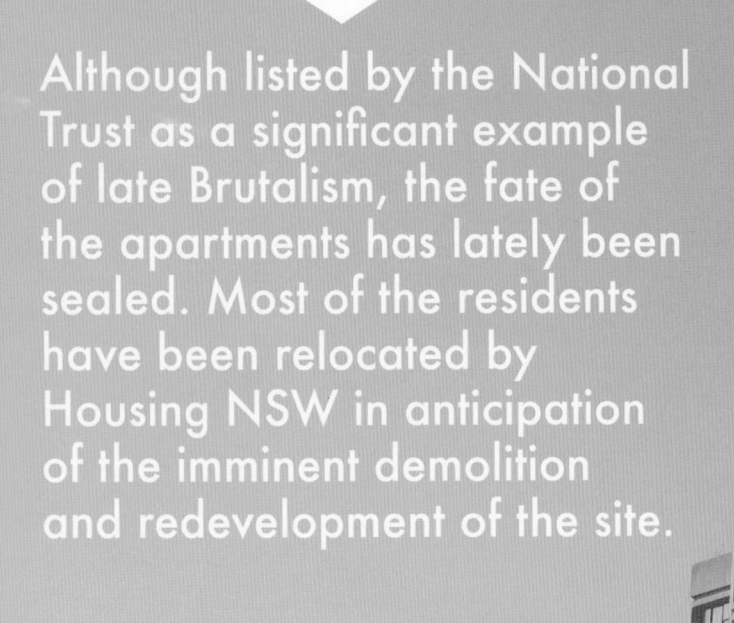

Although listed by the National Trust as a significant example of late Brutalism, the fate of the apartments has lately been sealed. Most of the residents have been relocated by Housing NSW in anticipation of the imminent demolition and redevelopment of the site.

33

Look across harbour
at McMahons Point

(8) McMahons Point / 1962 / Harry Seidler

BLUES POINT TOWER

Seidler's first major high rise project, Blues Point Tower has attracted an inordinate amount of criticism from Sydneysiders since its completion. In 1957 McMahons Point, now one of Sydney's most exclusive harbour-side suburbs, was being considered for industrial rezoning, motivating Seidler to put forward an alternative, and very Modernist, residential proposal. Reflecting architect Le Corbusier's theories regarding the future development of dense urban forms, Seidler planned a series of 28 high-rise towers for the area, all surrounded by landscaped gardens and commanding harbour views. Although the industrial rezoning ideas quickly fell out of favour any initial enthusiasm for the apartment project also rapidly waned and by 1962 Seidler had only managed to have one tower realised.

Rising 25 floors (Australia's tallest residential building until 1970) the tower is square in plan with brick clad facades and features interesting surface patterning. On the East-West elevations each floor is expressed by ribbon windows flanked by staggered balconies alternating on the right and left sides. The North-South facades have a similar layout with additional balcony elements running staggered up the middle. This aversion to unbroken symmetrical grids became a signature Seidler element and can be found on many of his subsequent tower projects.

From the beginning Blues Point Tower was decried by many as an eyesore completely at odds with its surroundings. In a Modernist sense, however, it should be considered an unmitigated success; A vertical urban form rising amongst the trees and lawns of Blues Point as a free-standing sculpture. As Seidler himself said: "I've always thought Blues Point Tower is one of my best buildings and I stand by that. Anybody who can't see anything in it ought to go back to school."

UNDER THREAT

Redevelopment is imminent.

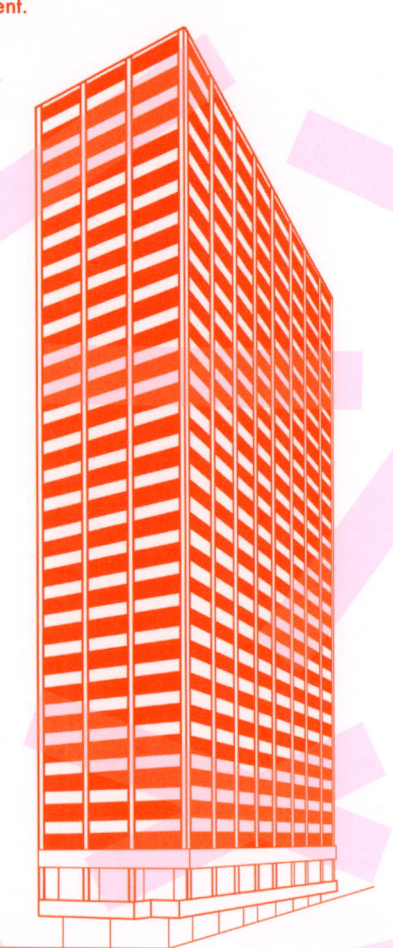

9 1 Alfred St / 1966 / Peddle Thorp and Walker

GOLD FIELDS HOUSE

Designed by the same architectural firm that produced the AMP Building, Gold Fields House (commissioned by British mining company Consolidated Gold Fields) demonstrates the evolution of the curtain wall throughout Australia during the 1960s. The coloured glass spandrels and light aluminium mullions have been replaced with composite materials and heavier forms, lending a more solid expressive appearance to the facades. Although reclad in the 1990s the building retains the original dimensions and contrasts of the grid form; wide spandrel bands running parallel to the ribbon windows are intersected with narrow strips at four pane intervals. The windows in each section are further divided equally by an opaque flush panel.

Gold Fields House was one of a series of freestanding skyscrapers that transformed Sydney's skyline in the 1960s and stands today as a neat, well-proportioned example of mid-century corporate architecture. Unfortunately it may soon be transformed beyond recognition having being purchased in 2014 with the intention of redevelopment into luxury accommodation.

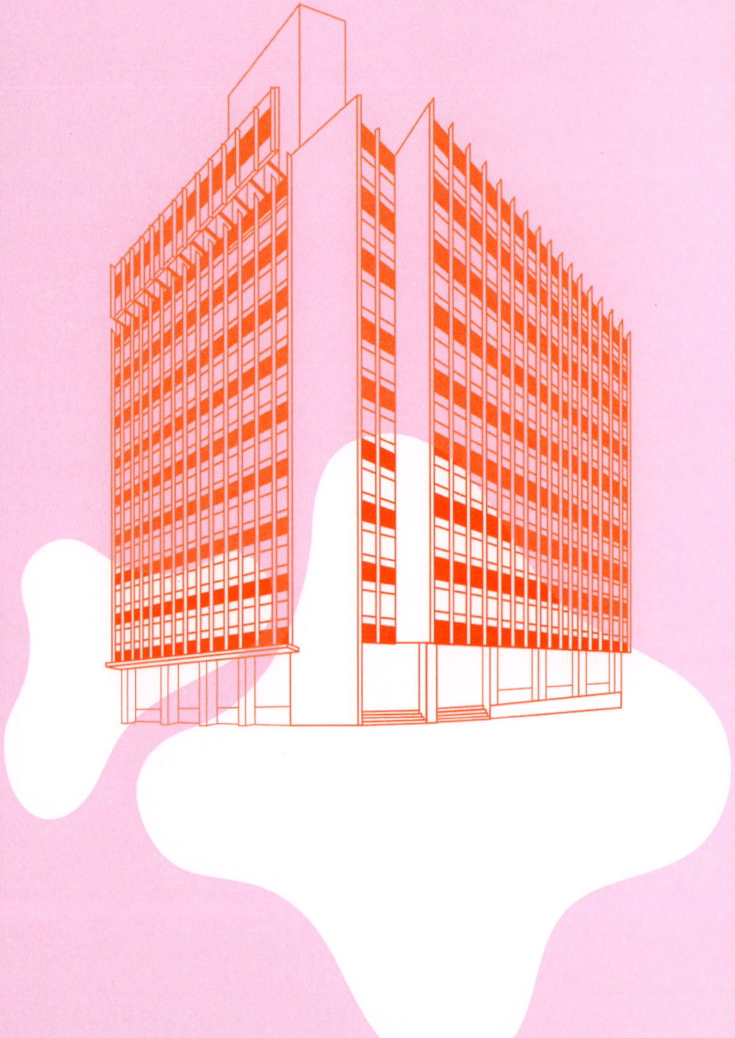

10 51 Pitt St / 1959 / Architect Unknown

51 PITT ST

Located on a corner site this 11 storey office building is a generally typical example of late 1950s curtain wall commercial design, with a couple of quirks. Two window rows in from the corner the Pitt Street facade extends outwards, coming in line with the adjacent building. The Dalley Street facade wraps around into the rear lane, giving the impression of a free-standing, full curtain wall structure. This is for effect only, however, as the windows terminate after two rows, the remaining wall taking the form of a brick warehouse. The facades themselves are made up of light blue spandrels separated by unbroken aluminium mullion fins, all of which sit above a colonnaded ground floor.

Overall the exterior of 51 Pitt Street is intact and, apart from the ground floor entrance level, is in quite original condition.

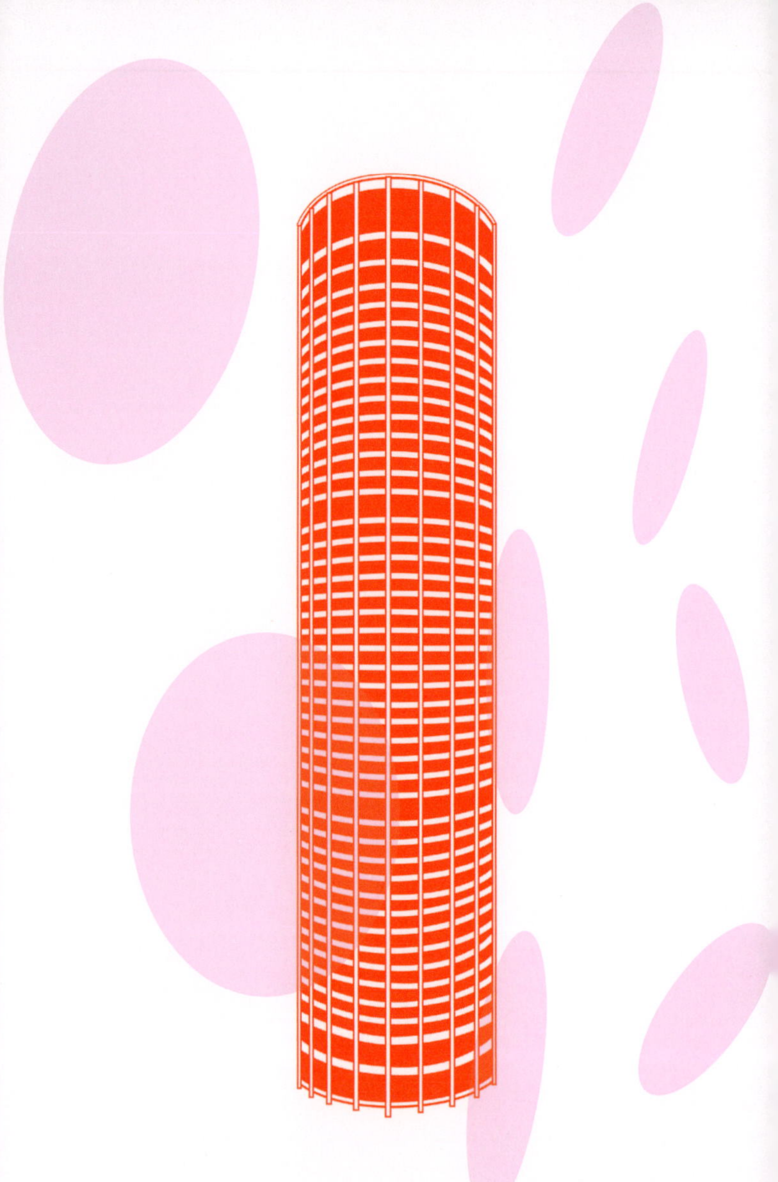

11 264 George St / 1967 / Harry Seidler

AUSTRALIA SQUARE

When completed in 1967 the Australia Square complex (comprising a 170 metre tower and 13 floor building, both sited on an open plaza) represented a new form of urban development in an Australian city. Occupying an entire city block (made possible by the acquisition and demolition of around 30 properties) the project sought to provide a less congested environment for city workers and pedestrians, being an early example of publically accessible open space situated on private land.

Construction commenced in 1962, the 13 floor Plaza Building on Pitt Street being completed first in order to provide rental income whilst the tower was constructed. Raised on angled concrete piloti the Plaza Building encloses one end of the space as well as defining the street edge.

Sited at the opposite end of the plaza is Australia Square Tower, a building regarded as one of Harry Seidler's greatest works of commercial architecture. In association with engineer Pier Luigi Nervi (known as the Italian god of concrete), Seidler devised the unique cylindrical form for both practical and aesthetic reasons. Given the relatively narrow site and council rules around building setbacks a circular design provided more floorplate space and occupied less of the site compared to a traditional rectangular building, in addition to providing better outward views. The structural nature of the building (a central round core with external structural columns) also results in uncluttered office space. Visually, the external column fins soaring past the prominent spandrel bands, draw the eye dramatically up the tower, at the top of which sits a revolving restaurant. The lobby interior is no less spectacular with its ceiling of interlocking ribs and colourful mural by New York artist Sol LeWitt wrapping around the central core.

Australia Square Tower is considered a milestone building in Australia's Modernist architectural history. Architectural photographer Patrick Bingham-Hall calls it "Australia's finest tall building, a perfect resolution of rational geometry, structural ingenuity and heroic form".

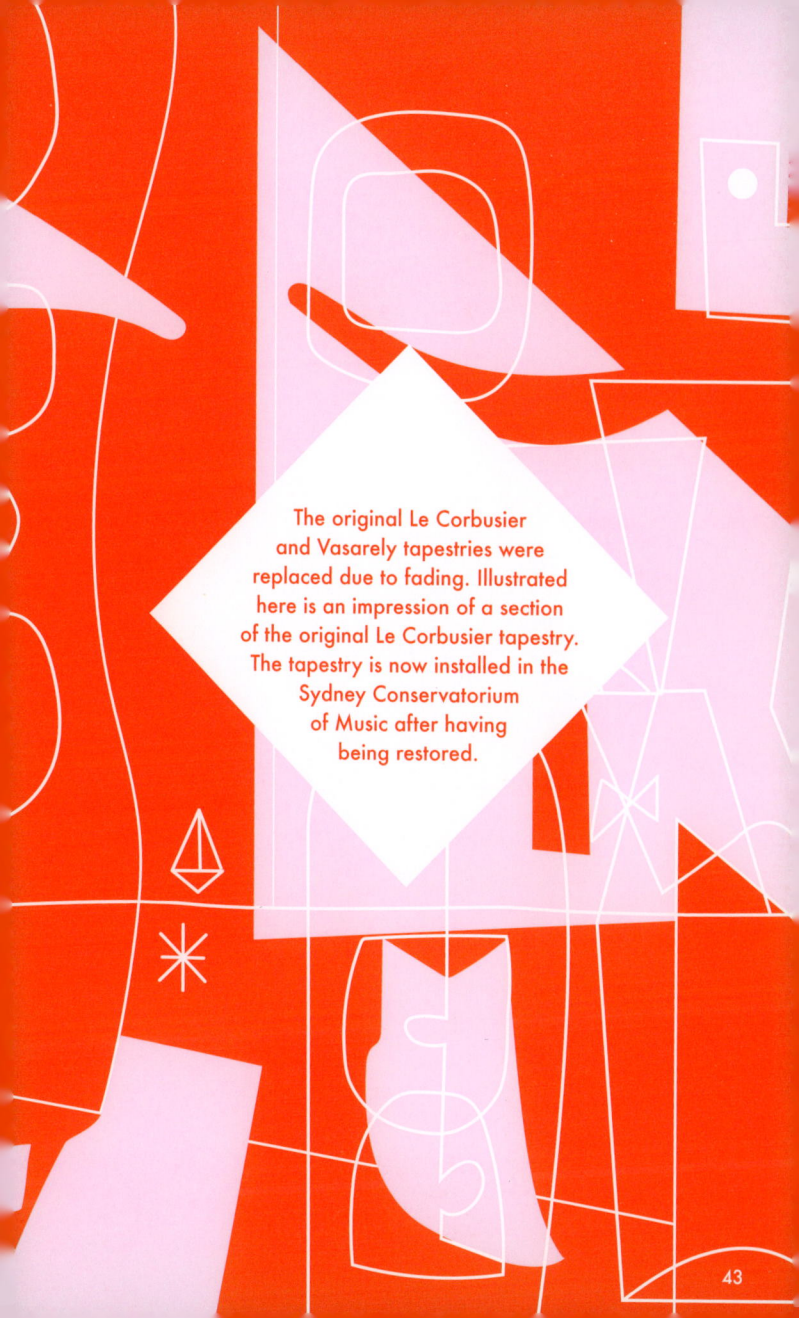

The original Le Corbusier and Vasarely tapestries were replaced due to fading. Illustrated here is an impression of a section of the original Le Corbusier tapestry. The tapestry is now installed in the Sydney Conservatorium of Music after having being restored.

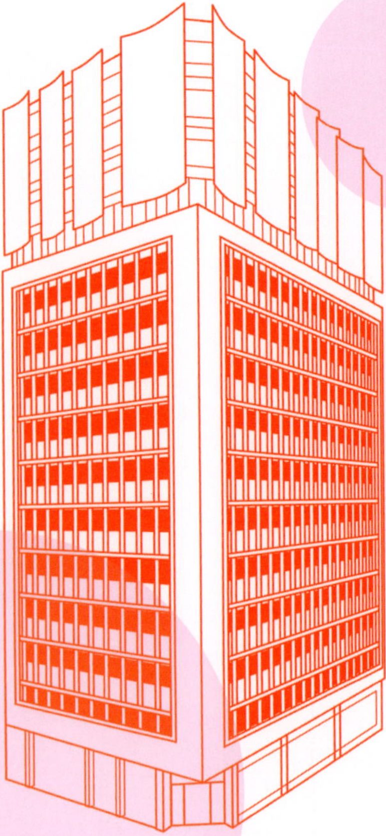

12 · 97 Pitt St / 1963 / Stafford Moor & Farrington

GUARDIAN ASSURANCE BUILDING

The early 1960s curtain wall design of this building demonstrates the tendency of architects at the time to develop a more 'expressive' form. The windows and spandrel elements are encased in a projecting grid which is itself framed in an expressed rectangle. The overall appearance is a little fussy and can be read as a transition between the clean aluminium and glazed skin of early International Style designs and the later, composite 'punched window' styles.

Originally constructed for the British Guardian Assurance Company (now AXA) the building was recently transformed into the Tank Stream boutique hotel. Apart from the addition of four extra floors the exterior form of the building was generally retained including the original cladding of locally sourced Wombeyan marble (no longer quarried). The hotel is named after the stream (now part of the sewerage system running under the city) that provided the early European settlers of Sydney with fresh water.

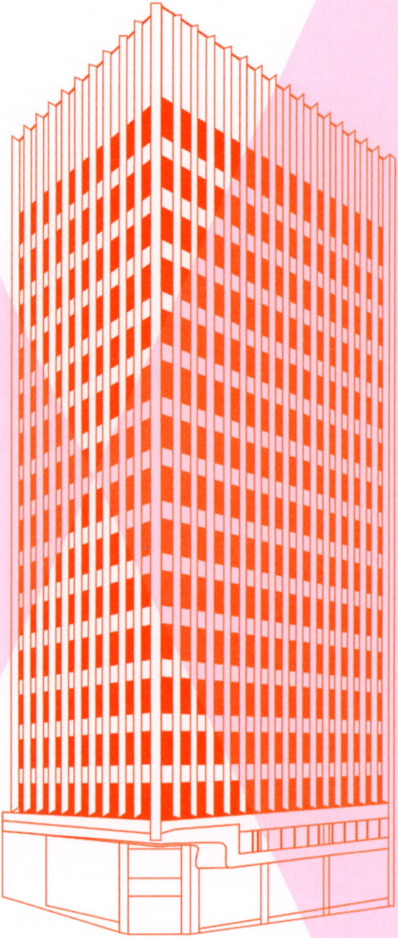

13 23 Hunter St / 1972 / Architect Unknown

CURRENCY HOUSE

Located in a prime CBD location on the corner of Pitt and Hunter Streets, Currency House appears ostensibly to be a typical early 1970s composite curtain wall design. On closer inspection however the overall facade treatment alludes more to the machine age forms of Art Deco architecture.

The triangular mullion elements run the length of the building, terminating past the top floor windows and providing a repetitive serrated edge pattern when viewed from street level. The spandrels display equally repetitive patterns of lines which add to the decorative verticality of the design. Clad in tan coloured composite stone Currency House presents as a well-proportioned and subtly elegant structure that sets itself apart other office buildings of the era.

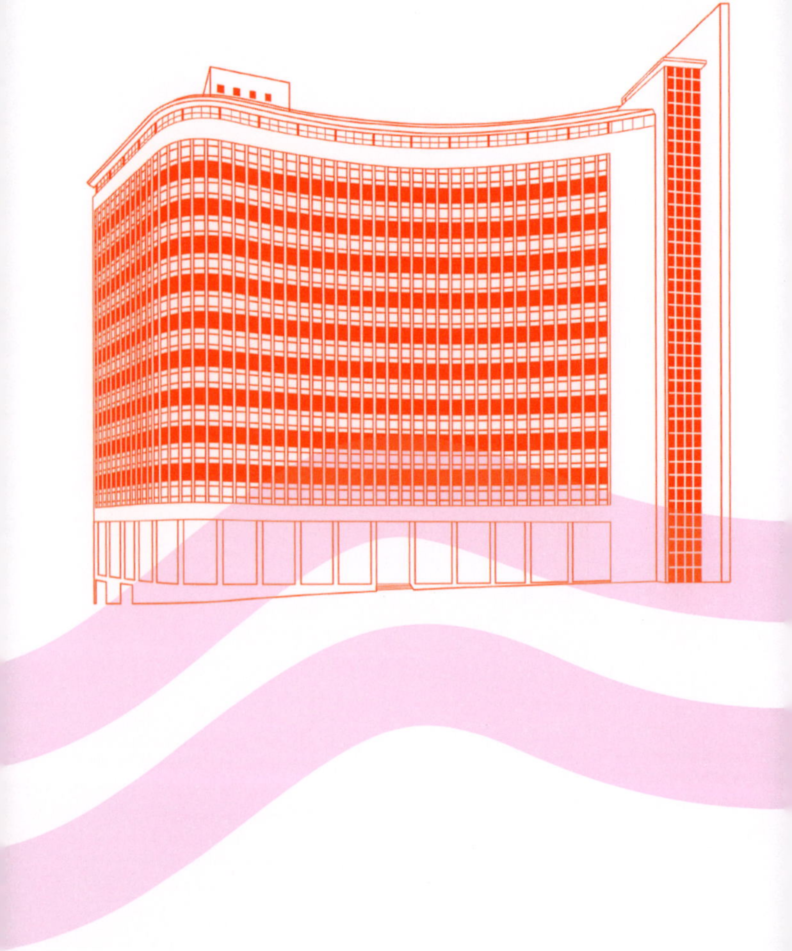

14 1 Chifley Square / 1957 / Rudder Littlemore & Rudder

QANTAS HOUSE

Officially opened by Prime Minister Robert Menzies on October 28th, 1957, Qantas House was the first purpose-built headquarters for what was then known as Qantas Empire Airways, Australia's sole international airline.

The third oldest airline in the world (established in 1920 as 'Queensland and Northern Territory Aerial Services Limited'), Qantas had greatly expanded its services in the post war years and by the 1950s was flying to multiple destinations around the globe. The international nature of the business was reflected in the International Style of the new building with its use of a broad aluminium and glass curtain wall, increasingly utilised at the time as the face of corporate architecture throughout the world.

What distinguishes Qantas House from other contemporary office designs is the form the architects used to express this new engineering technology. The facade follows the curved edge of Chifley Square, wrapping around to meet Hunter Street before terminating at Emil Sodersten's 1936 City Mutual Life Building. The green glazing and deep blue enamelled spandrels are intersected by aerofoil shaped aluminium mullions, all of which are framed by a contrasting border of local sandstone. Located above the sandstone band is a recessed rooftop level that originally contained staff and recreational facilities. The 11 office levels sit above a double height foyer clad in polished black granite with large, bronze-framed windows.

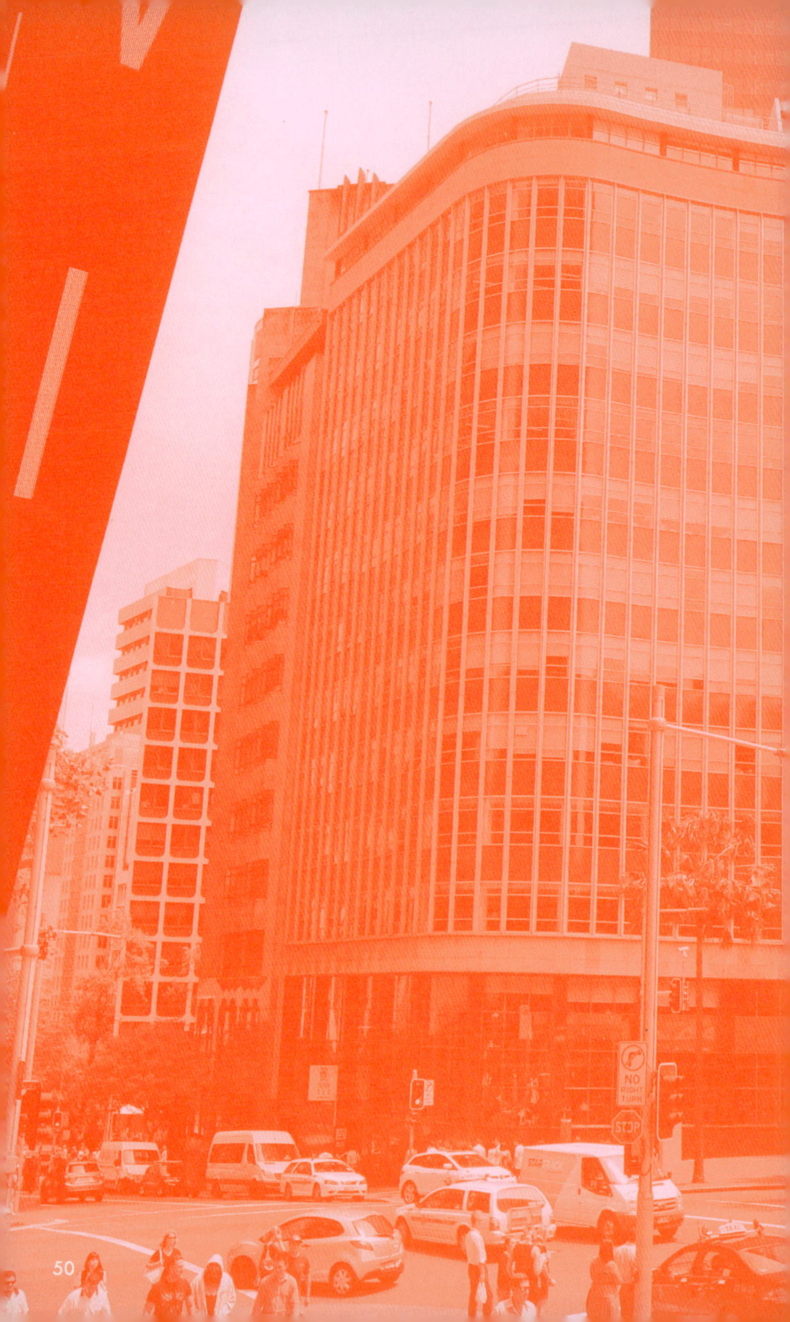
NO
RIGHT
TURN
STOP

Judged the best new building in the British Commonwealth by the Royal Institute of British Architects in 1959, Qantas House is still regarded as one of Sydney's finest curtain wall designs of the 1950s and is currently listed on the NSW State Heritage Register.

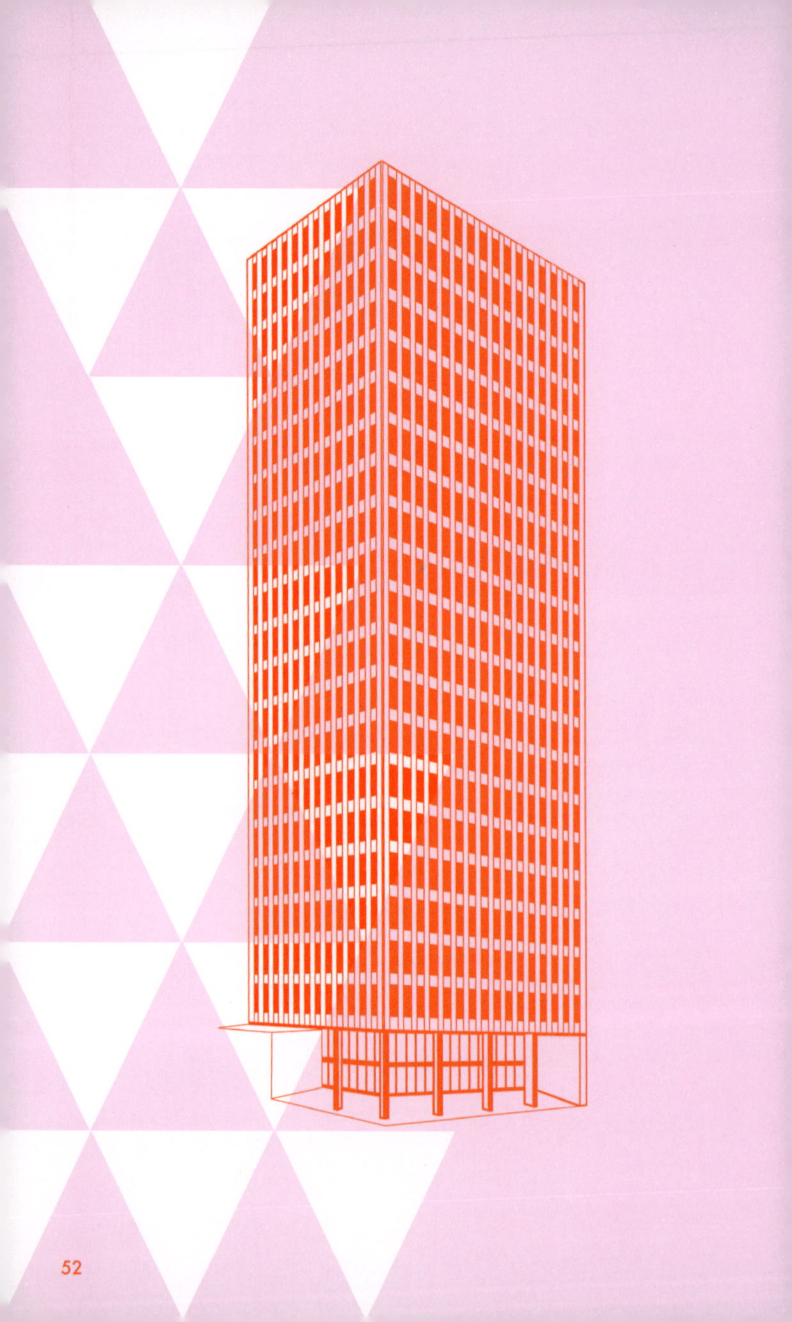

15 1 Castlereagh St / 1964 / Stephenson & Turner

PEARL ASSURANCE BUILDING

Originally constructed for the Pearl Assurance Company of London, 1 Castlereagh Street is a neatly designed office building with an interesting surface treatment. The ground and first levels are set back to form a colonnade above which the building rises 20 floors.

The mullion elements, faced with cream marble, provide a stark contrast to the dark bronze stone cladding (locally quarried polished trachyte) of the spandrels and columns. The aluminium framed windows project beyond the spandrels and the use of dark glazing further enhances the overall contrasting quality of the facade surfaces.

The building was one of the first in Sydney to incorporate new window technology that enabled each panel to pivot around an axis, allowing easy cleaning from the inside. In addition, internal venetian blinds were sandwiched between the double glazing of each panel.

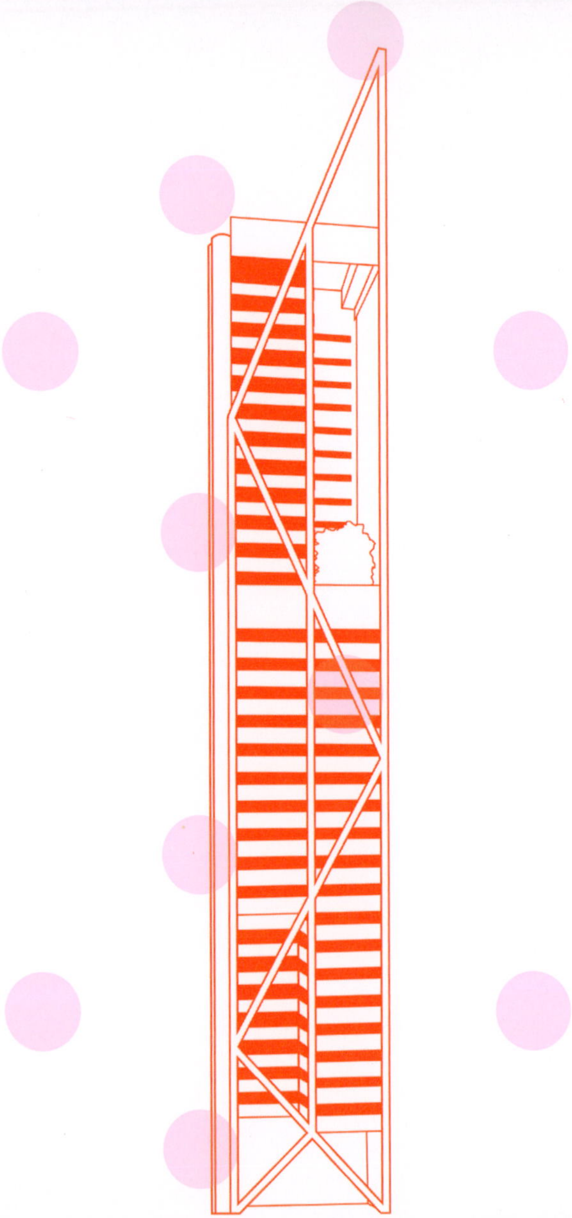

16 9-11 Castlereagh St / 1989 / Harry Seidler

CAPITA CENTRE

Although constrained by a tight, restricted site Harry Seidler managed to produce a building expressing many of his design hallmarks that would otherwise require a much larger space. The architect used the irregular site shape to his advantage by placing the core and main lift shaft at the perimeter, leaving a clear rectangular space for the tower.

This provided more open, flexible floor space on each level than would be possible with a central core. Creating voids throughout the structure also enabled maximum natural light to penetrate the floors, starting with the publically accessible open space at ground level.

The trade-off for all this, however, was a reduction in overall lateral stiffness which resulted in what is probably the most dramatic structural feature of the building, the exposed truss on the facade. A zig-zag framed in vertical elements, the truss soars up the tower carrying the eye through the alternating spaces of voids and louvered surfaces.

Terminating at a flag pole (which brings the height of the building to 183 metres) this external support feature places the Capita Centre firmly in the High-Tech Structural Expressionist school of modern architecture.

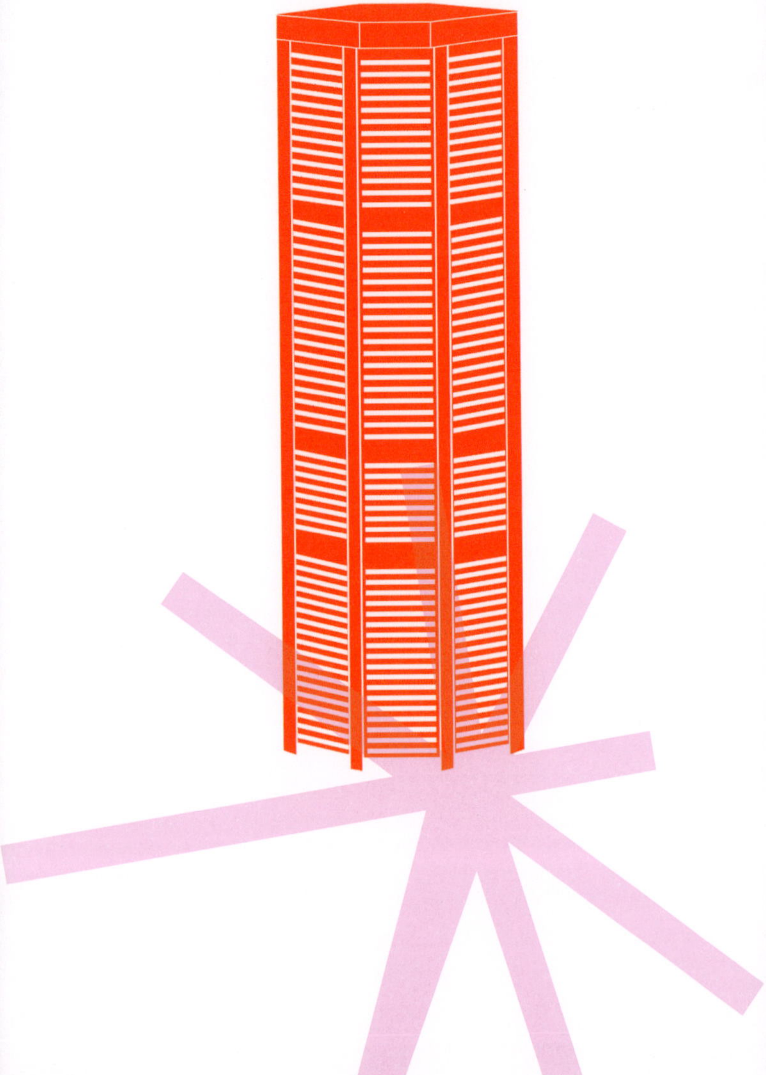

17 19 Martin Place / 1977 / Harry Seidler

MLC CENTRE

Completed exactly ten years after his seminal Australia Square project, Seidler's MLC Centre saw an evolution and refining of the architect's urban planning ideas. Teaming up once again with Italian engineer Pier Luigi Nervi (whose beautiful concrete geometric patterns can be seen in the ceilings of many of the structures), Seidler designed an open plaza comprising a 67 storey tower surrounded by retail, arts and recreation facilities, reflecting his belief in providing uncongested central urban space for city workers and pedestrians. The tower has an octagonal floorplan with a central core and is structurally supported by eight massive external columns that taper towards the top of the building. The office windows are recessed from the horizontal beam spandrels, providing both sun shading and a heavier textural quality to the surface. As it only occupies 20 percent of the site, the tower (Australia's tallest building until 1985) seems an integral, not over-bearing, feature of the complex.

The plaza is arranged on podiums of differing levels on which are placed various structures, circular in form, that relate spatially to the tower in an almost organic manner. A large central well admits natural light to the shopping arcades below whilst the distinctive mushroom shaped structure on the North East corner is home to the Commercial Travellers' Association's Business Club. The Theatre Royal, Australia's oldest theatrical institution, is also part of the complex, the original theatre building (opened in 1875) having been demolished, along with the Australia Hotel (1889), to clear the site for the MLC Centre. As with all of Seidler's commercial projects, contemporary artwork features prominently and includes the bright yellow 'S' sculpture by Charles Perry (located on the top level of the piazza) and "New Constellation", by Robert Owen (hanging on the tower foyer wall).

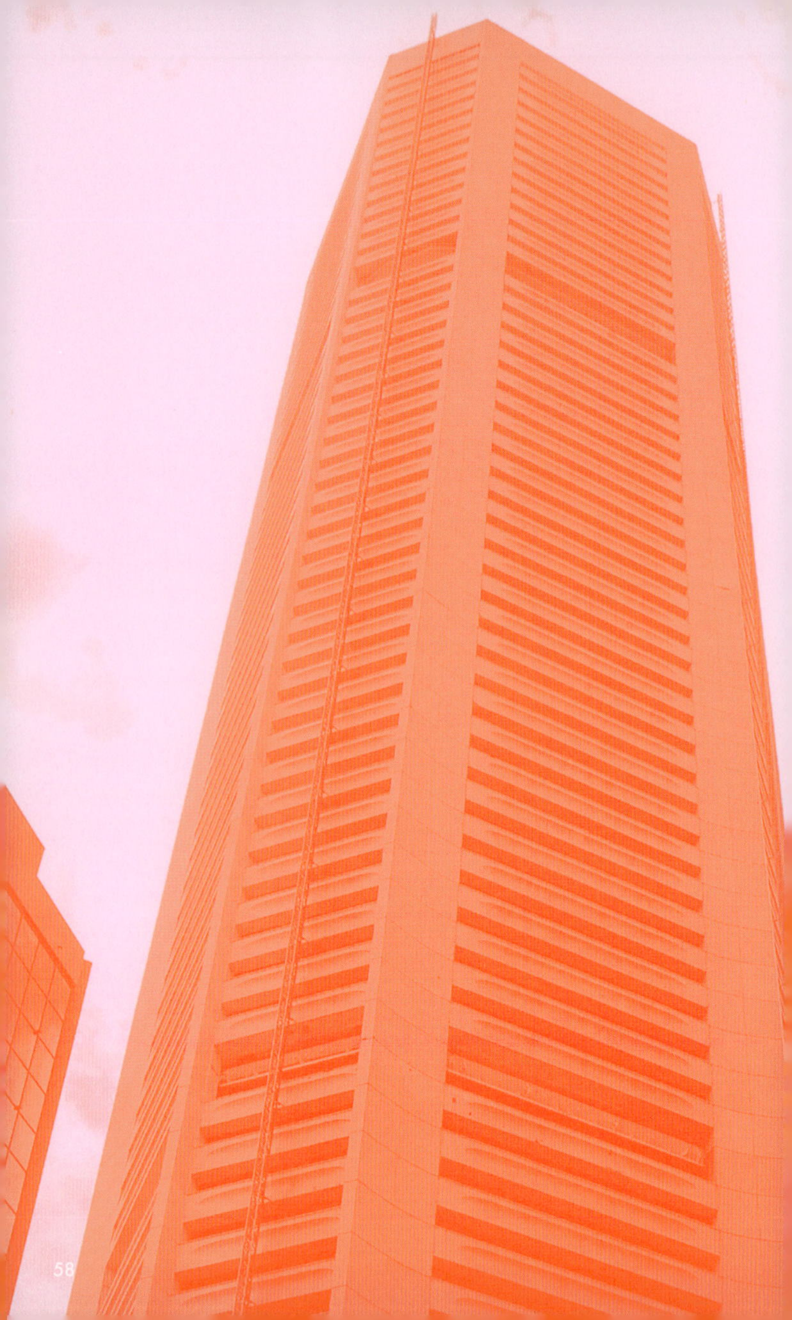

A thriving hub in Sydney's business precinct, the MLC Centre was further confirmation of Harry Seidler's pre-eminence as a designer of finely crafted and sensitive built forms within often harsh and uncompromising urban environments.

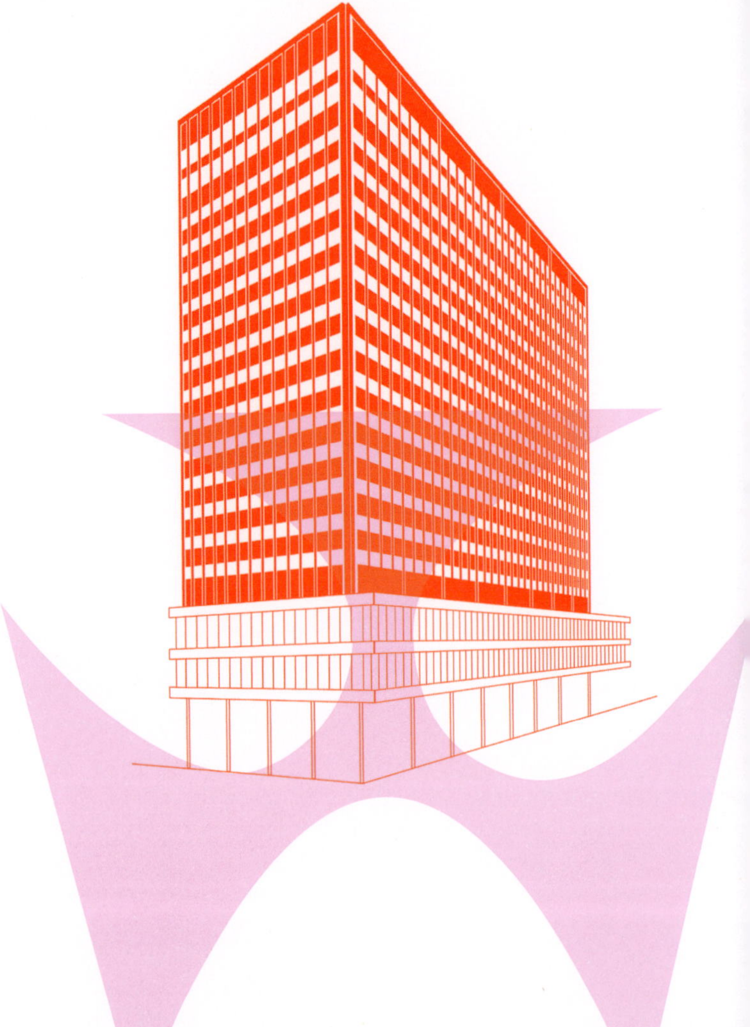

18 65 Martin Place / 1964 / Commonwealth Department of Works

RESERVE BANK BUILDING

Established as Australia's central bank on 14th of January, 1960, construction of a new Sydney office for the Reserve Bank commenced in 1961. The bank's administrators made it clear that the new design should be contemporary and international, reflecting the post-war cultural shifts of the nation. They also insisted on the use of high quality Australian sourced materials for construction and Australian art for decoration. The resulting design comprised a four-storey podium topped by a sixteen-storey tower. The double height ground level, entered via a granite terrace, is recessed and fully glazed whilst the two floors above project outwards on horizontal platforms.

The tower is composed of curtain wall facades clad with locally sourced black granite mullions and cream marble spandrels (4 panels each). Square aluminium windows puncture the surface and are recessed for sun shading, with additional projecting shades on the west elevation. At the top level are eight bays defined by the extended granite mullion elements which in turn become column supports.

Apart from furnishings and some fittings the foyer interior is largely original. Eight gold anodised-metal panels line the ceiling and the rear wall, clad in the same Wombeyan marble as the exterior, is decorated with an abstract sculpture by Bim Hilder. Another sculpture by Australian-American artist Margel Hinder sits in the Martin Place forecourt.

✪ OF NOTE

Sydney Law School Building / 1969 / 173 Philip Street

Sitting opposite the Law Courts building on Phillip Street is an earlier, far more expressive example of Brutalist architecture. Columns stack up the facades like blocks delineating the location of each floor. The windows, grouped into sets of four over a shared projecting spandrel, are shaded with horizontal fin elements that alternate in spacing from the lower floors to the top. Constructed as Sydney University's law faculty campus, the school has now relocated to a new building and, at the time of writing, the Philip Street structure was slated for demolition.

Utilising locally produced materials and art the Reserve Bank building demonstrated both Australian technological and cultural prowess that, in turn, reflected a heightened notion of self-reliance and confidence that was being felt in the post-war years.

The sense that the nation was now an independent, mature country, free from any colonial ties, was further enhanced by the change from British derived pounds, shillings and pence to a decimal currency system in 1966, all overseen, of course, by the Reserve Bank of Australia.

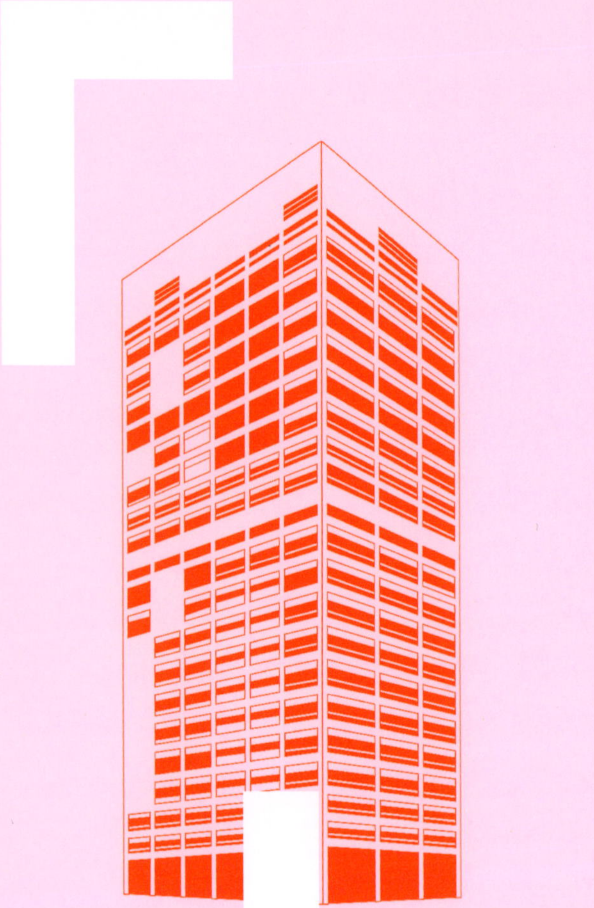

19 · 184 Phillip St / 1976 / McConnel, Smith & Johnson

LAW COURTS BUILDING

Housing the High and Federal Courts of Australia and the Supreme Court of NSW, the Law Courts building is a strong, sober design that befits its crucial role in Australia's legal system. The building's prestige is further emphasised by its location on Queens Square, around which some of Sydney's earliest administrative and civic architecture stands, including the Mint (1816), St James Church (1824) and the old Supreme Court building (1828).

The building is a prime example of the Brutalist style as it had developed in Australia throughout the late 1960s and 70s, particularly when applied to administrative and academic architecture. Clad in pre-cast concrete, the facades are lifted three storeys above the entrance foyer on slim columns before settling into a pattern of strip windows and blank panels. This informs the function of the internal spaces as open offices and closed courtrooms, with added textural interest provided by horizontal concrete sunshades.

A building that clearly demonstrates its purpose whilst responding to local environmental conditions, the Law Courts building is a typically pragmatic expression of 1970s regional Brutalist architecture.

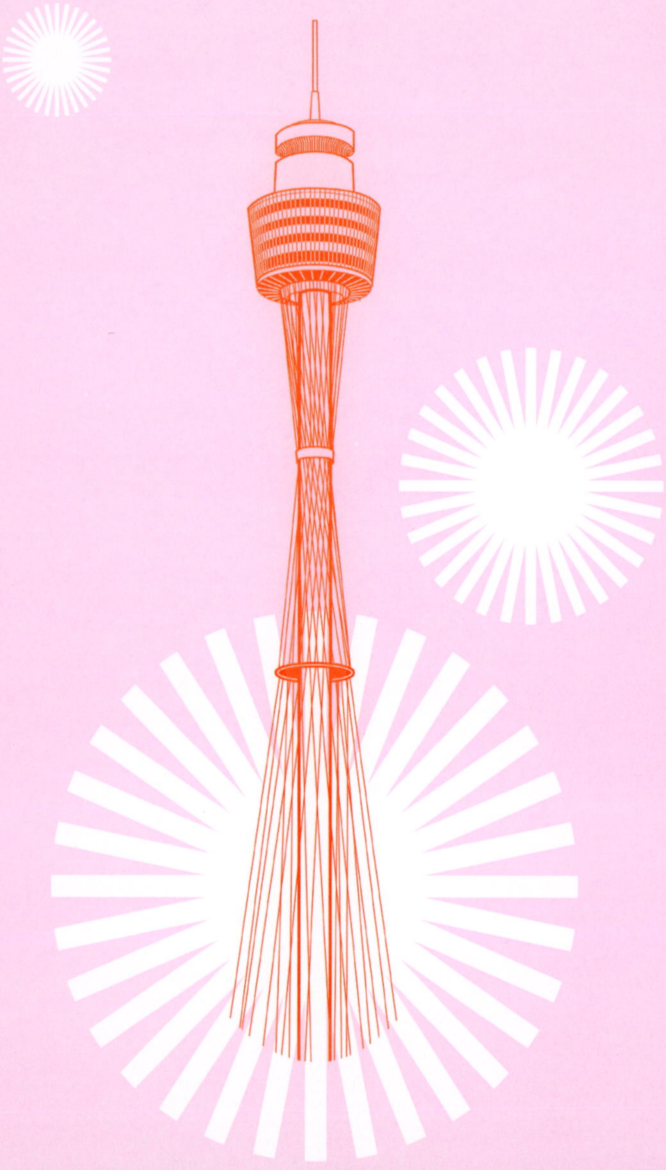

20 Pitt & Martin Sts / 1981 / Donald Crone

CENTREPOINT

At 309 metres (including spire) Sydney Tower is the city's tallest freestanding structure. Sitting above the Westfield shopping centre building, construction of the tower commenced in 1975 and it was opened to the public in 1981. The supporting shaft consists of 46 barrel-shaped units (each weighing 27 tonnes) topped by the multi-level turret structure.

The welded steel frame turret was fabricated at the base and gradually raised to the top as construction of the shaft proceeded. Braced by 56 steel cables, forming a hyperboloid shape, the tower was designed to withstand winds in excess of 260kph and includes a 162,000 litre water tank in the turret to serve as a counterbalance. The 'golden basket' as it is known has a capacity for 960 people and includes an observation deck, two revolving restaurants, and two active telecommunication transmission levels.

A further external viewing platform above the turret, added in 2005, provides an extra thrill for those with the nerve.

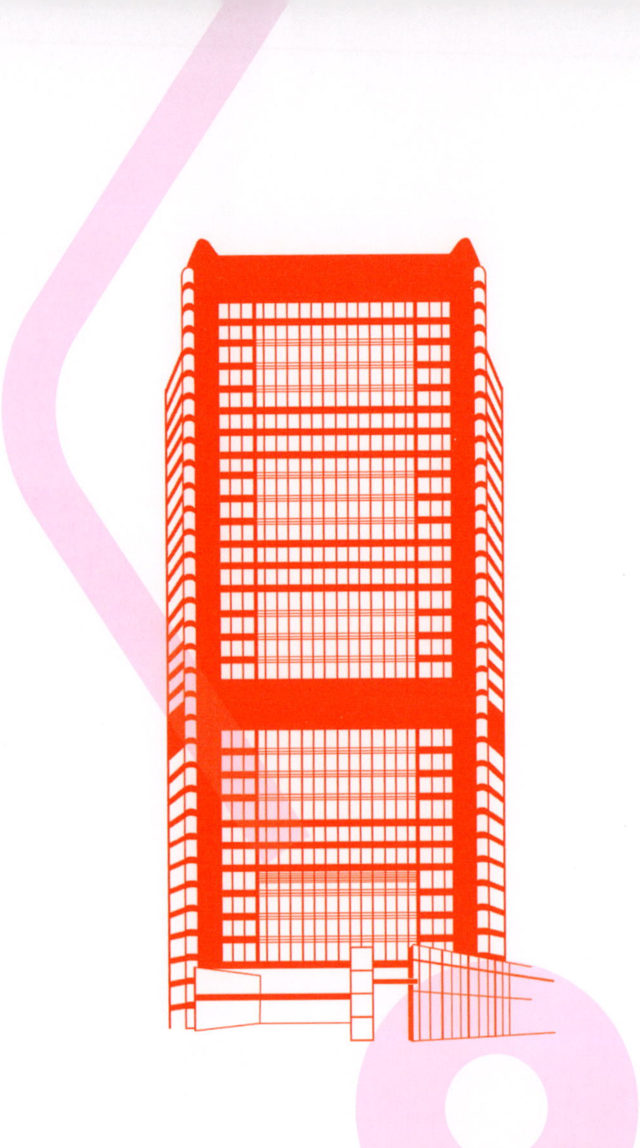

21 Corner 378-394 George St / 1976 / John Andrews

KING GEORGE BUILDING

Now referred to simply as 388 George Street, the building situated on one of Sydney's busiest intersections has long been regarded as an iconic example of 1970s Brutalist/High Tech architecture. Triangular in shape, the three glass facades are flanked by circular stairway and lift cores, dramatically expressed externally in off-form concrete. To provide relief from the harsh solar conditions Andrews applied a system of polycarbonate sunshades hung off an intricate space frame lattice, giving the glazed facades what many considered a lively and delicate quality that relieved somewhat the harsh structural concrete finishes. Renovations during the 1990s, however, saw the removal of the lattice frame system, partly to satisfy the new tenants' (NRMA Insurance) desire for increased natural light and unimpeded city views. Environmental control is now performed by sensor-equipped glass panels which help ventilate the five sky gardens (expressed on the facade as five aluminium-framed rectangles) incorporated into the new design.

What some see as a degradation of the building's original unique character, others consider an appropriate renewing and upgrading of a technological system, allowing a significant architectural example to exist in an overall intact form for many years to come.

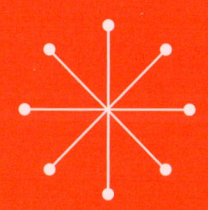

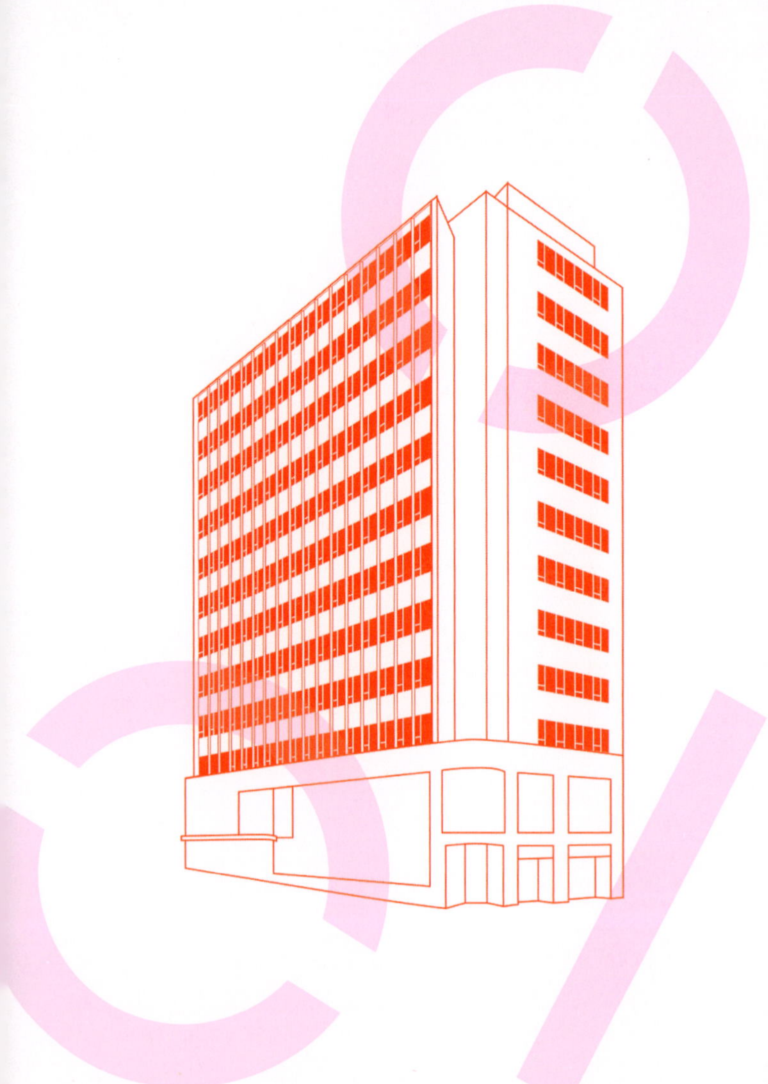

22 423-427 George St / 1956 / Commonwealth Department of Works

COMMONWEALTH BANK BUILDING

The site on which the Commonwealth Bank building stands today was purchased in 1939, although construction didn't commence until 1954 due to World War 2 and the post-war widening of Market Street. The eventual 12 storey design was therefore narrower than intended, resulting in three separate banking chambers occupying the lower ground, ground and first floors, all linked by escalators. This, along with the air-conditioning system (distributed to each level through perforated metal ceiling tiles), was an innovative feature for Sydney office buildings at the time.

The building is comprised of a two-storey podium, re-clad in polished granite in the 1990s, upon which sit ten floors of office space finished in the original sandstone. The Market Street elevation is dominated by an aluminium and glass curtain wall that projects from the facade within a sandstone frame. Each window is divided into unequal thirds with vertically ribbed spandrels adding to the textural nature of the surface.

The inclusion of public art was an important consideration from the beginning of the project and the three works originally displayed on the exterior survive intact. On the York Street elevation is a sandstone relief by sculptor Gerald Francis Lewers (1905-1962), whilst two works by Lyndon Dadswell (1908-1986) adorn the Market and George Street facades.

Not only was the Commonwealth Bank building the first major office tower to be constructed after World War 2, it is also the earliest remaining intact curtain wall structure in Sydney's CBD.

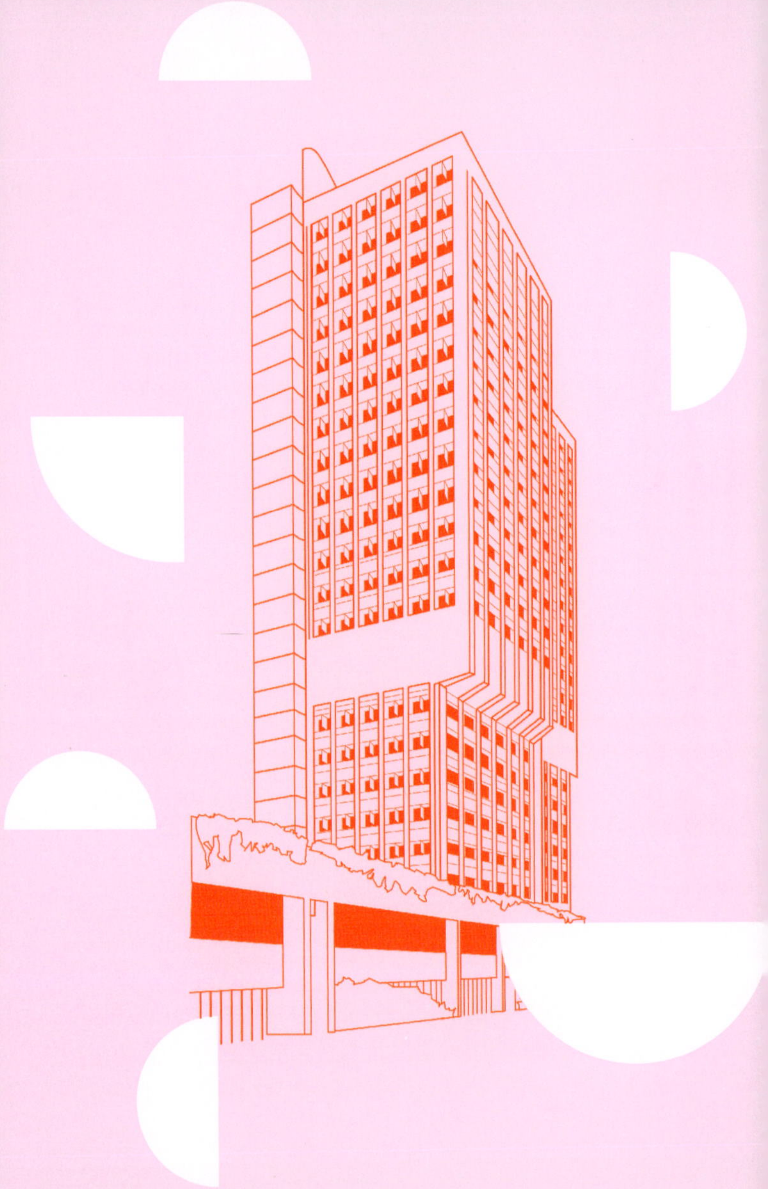

Town Hall Square / 1977 / Ancher Mortlock and Woolley

TOWN HALL HOUSE

Since the 1880s the grand Town Hall building, sited on the corner of George and Druitt Streets, has been the seat of local government for the City of Sydney. By the 1970s, however, both the city and council had grown to such an extent that staff were scattered throughout the CBD. A new building was proposed to both centralise administration and improve the efficiency of the organisation.

Opened in 1977, Town Hall House is sited directly behind the Town Hall building on the corner of Druitt and Kent Streets. A stark contrast to its intricately decorated Victorian neighbour, the new building nonetheless reflected the architectural trends of its time with its complex stacked forms executed in the Brutalist manner.

Sitting on a multi-level podium the structure is essentially three main towers formed around a common service core. Rising to 25 floors, each tower structure is made up of two distinct blocks; a six storey 'base' on which sits a further block that extends up and projects out on blade-like columns. Blade forms feature throughout the structure, used as vertical sun shading elements on the Kent Street elevation and throughout the podium structure. The windows are deeply recessed behind modular concave spandrel and frame elements.

Although unmistakably a product of 1970s Brutalism the architects were sensitive enough, given the spatial relationship to the older building, to give Town Hall House an acid-washed, buff-coloured aggregate finish that closely matches worn sandstone.

Be sure to check out the impressive scale model of the city on display in the ground floor foyer of Town Hall House.

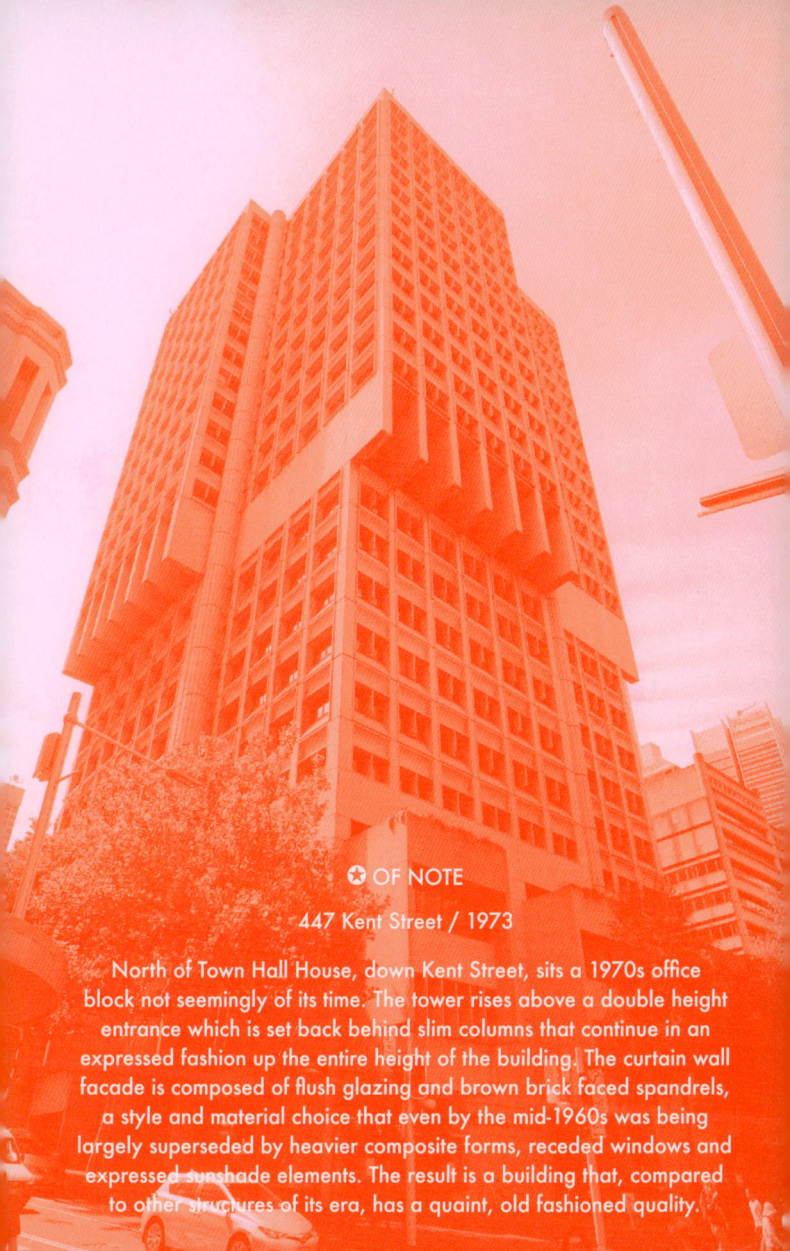

✪ OF NOTE

447 Kent Street / 1973

North of Town Hall House, down Kent Street, sits a 1970s office block not seemingly of its time. The tower rises above a double height entrance which is set back behind slim columns that continue in an expressed fashion up the entire height of the building. The curtain wall facade is composed of flush glazing and brown brick faced spandrels, a style and material choice that even by the mid-1960s was being largely superseded by heavier composite forms, receded windows and expressed sunshade elements. The result is a building that, compared to other structures of its era, has a quaint, old fashioned quality.

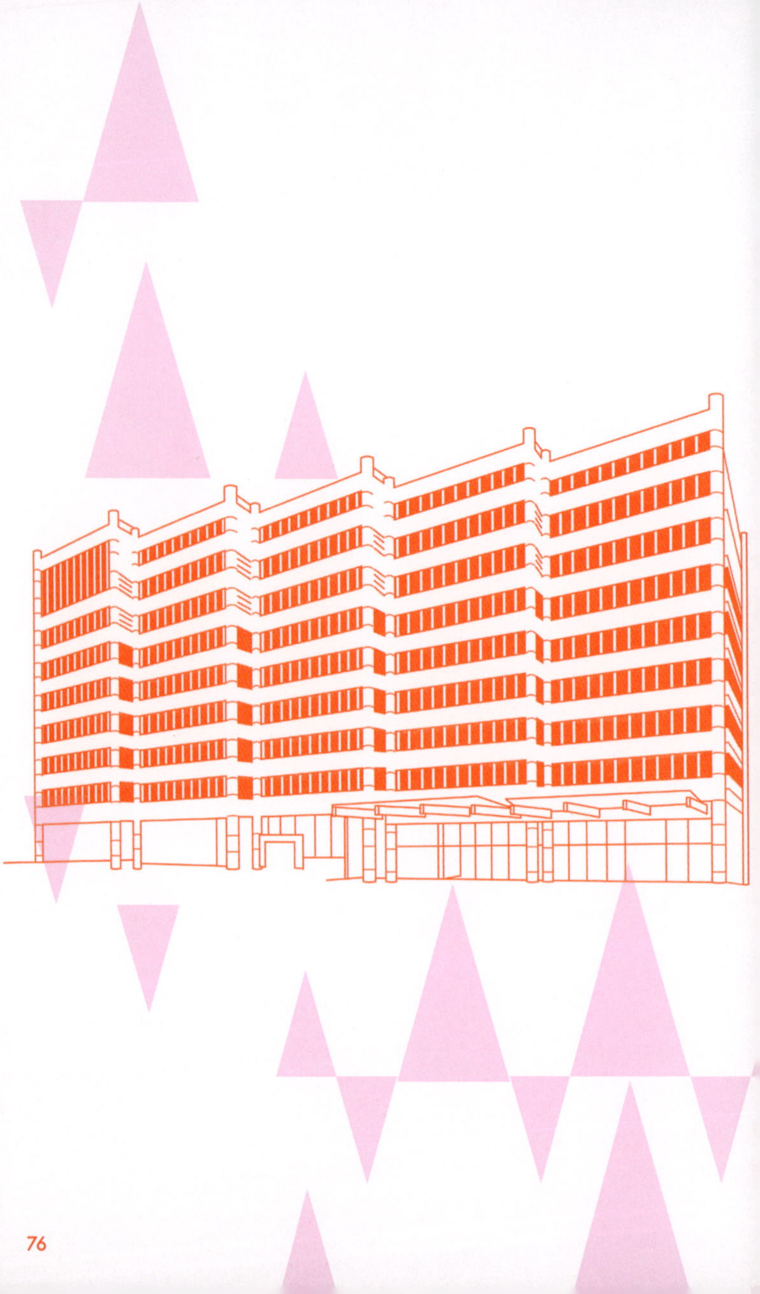

24 Town Hall Square / 1976 / Bell & Herbert F Hely

ST ANDREWS HOUSE

Completed a year before Town Hall House, St Andrews House is another Brutalist product of the 1970s, although representing a more sober version of the style. Providing office space for a number of tenants, the building was primarily designed as the new home for St Andrews Cathedral School, a private Anglican co-educational institution that was established in 1885. The state's first high rise school, it occupies the ground, 5th, 6th, 7th and 8th floors and is attended by 1,100 students from kindergarten to Year 12.

The complex is made up of five staggered structures raised above a double height ground floor on columns. The columns form the sides of each facade, interlocking with the ends of the thick horizontal bands that form the spandrel elements on each level. Receded ribbon windows sit behind the spandrels, divided into 11 panels by brown mullions. The top levels display divided apertures matching the windows below and form a boundary for the school's rooftop play area, providing a safe, open space in a congested city location.

Finished in a rough aggregate, St Andrew's House is somewhat typical of the Brutalist style institutional architecture that could be found on campuses around Australia throughout the 1970s and 80s.

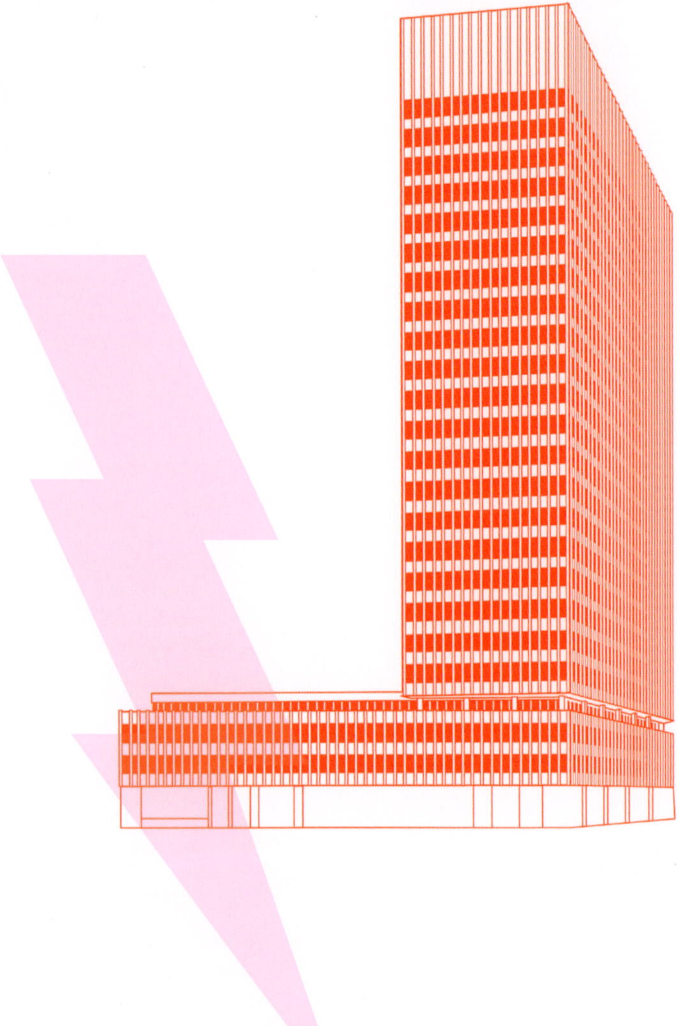

(25) Cnr Bathurst & George Sts / 1968 / Fowell, Mansfield & Maclurcan

SYDNEY ELECTRICITY BUILDING

The Sydney County Council building later renamed Sydney Electricity was opened in 1968. It offered a sharp contrast in architectural style to its previous premises, the 1898 Queen Victoria Building. Sited on an elevated podium the 20 storey tower dramatically delineates the George and Bathurst Streets corner on which it is located.

Due to its black expressed mullion forms and dark grey cladding the building has often been referred to as a 'Miesien black box', alluding to the work of German/American architect Ludwig Mies van der Rohe. A pioneer of the corporate International Style, his skyscrapers (such as the Seagram Building, N.Y, 1958) often exhibited signature elements of dark glass and flat black painted structural expressions.

In 1961, shortly before construction was commenced on the new building, the City Council announced plans to demolish the Queen Victoria Building, a decision that faced surprisingly little opposition from the public. The council was unable, however, to legally evict the Sydney County Council at the time and, in the ensuing seven year delay, sentiments concerning built heritage dramatically changed, saving the QVB from the wrecking ball.

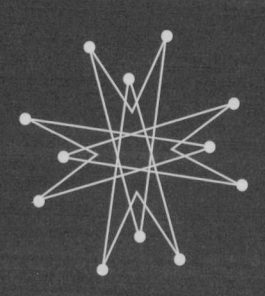

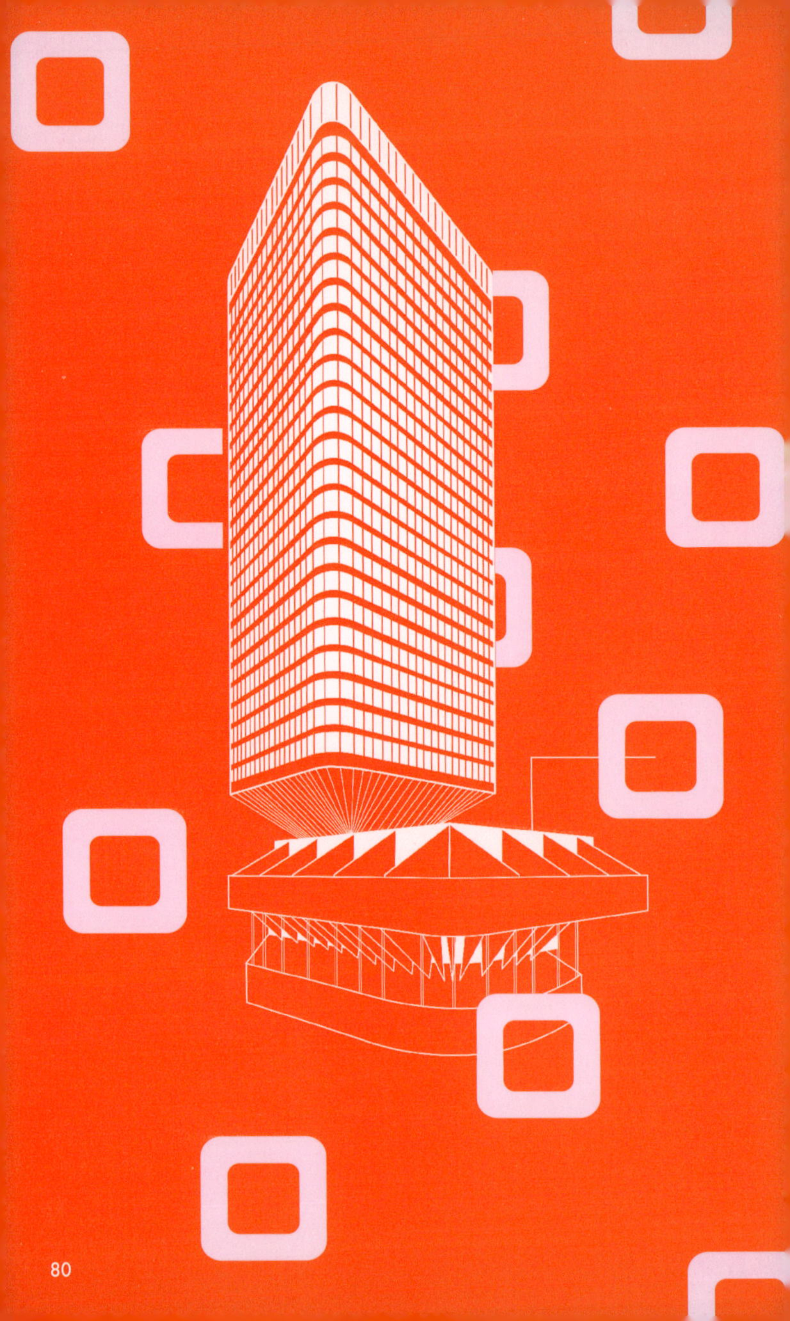

26 66 Goulburn St / 1974-2004 / Joseland Gilling

SYDNEY MASONIC CENTRE

Freemasonry came to Australia shortly after the arrival of the First Fleet in 1788. Initially composed mainly of British soldiers, civilians soon swelled the membership ranks and the first official Grand Lodge was opened in Sydney in 1845.

Opening in 1974 as the new headquarters for the United Grand Lodge of NSW and the ACT, the Sydney Masonic Centre was as controversial to some as the secretive society it represented. Initially lacking the tower component (included in the original design but not added until 2004) the original squat, Brutalist structure was essentially a 30 metre high concrete podium encircled by a broad platform structure. This was supported both above and below by a series of triangular buttress forms.

Thirty years after completion the Grocon construction company, which now owned the airspace above the centre, went forward with a plan to build a tower atop the existing structure. Rejecting plans for a contemporary 'glass box', the company decided to use the original 35 floor Joseland Gilling design. Fully supported on the central lift core Civic Tower, with its upward tapering base, seems to balance precariously above the podium, giving it a sense of lightness belying its heavy concrete from.

⊛ OF NOTE

Roden Cutler House / 1975 / 24 Campbell Street

Walk south down Pitt Street for a block and turn right into Campbell Street and you will find a building named after decorated World War 2 veteran and long serving NSW Governor (1966-1981), Sir Roden Cutler. One for the die-hard Brutalist fans, the building is typical of the 1970s take on the style with a blank street frontage rising six floors above the entrance, abruptly transitioning to a heavily sun louvered tower.

Although critics remain steadfast in their attacks on 1970s era Brutalist architecture, fans of the style have praised the sympathetic stylistic unification of the Masonic Centre and, as Dr Harry Margalit, (architecture lecturer at the University of Sydney) has said, "Without doubt there will come a time when it is loved, and I think that time is not far away".

ABOUT THE ARCHITECTS

Harry Seidler (1923-2006)

If not for a request from his mother Harry Seidler may have continued to forge his career as an architect in the United States.

Born in Vienna to Jewish parents, 14 year old Seidler was sent to England soon after the Nazi occupation of Austria in 1938. In 1940 he was studying building and construction at Cambridgeshire Technical School when, because of his Austrian background, he was interned as an enemy alien on the Isle of Man. Shipped off to Quebec, Canada, his detention continued until October, 1941 when he was given probational release to study architecture at the University of Manitoba in Winnipeg. Graduating in 1944, Seidler was registered as an architect in 1945, becoming a Canadian citizen the following year.

He went on to study under Bauhaus founder Walter Gropius at the Harvard School of Design and subsequently worked for various architectural luminaries including Alvar Alto, Oscar Niemeyer and Marcel Breuer. An avid student of Modernist design principles from early on, the tuition and experience gained from these associations further cemented Seidler's convictions and ambitions concerning architecture and influenced many aspects of his own work. Breuer's 'bi-nuclear' house forms can be seen in Seidler's early timber domestic projects whilst sun shading elements and use of curved concrete forms, as utilised by Niemeyer, are evident in many of his later commercial towers.

Siedler's parents had migrated to Australia in 1946, settling in Sydney. In 1947 Rose Seidler contacted her son in New York with an interesting request: visit his parents and design a new home for them. The 'Rose Seidler House' as it has become known was completed in 1950 and, with its clearly Bauhaus-derived design philosophies expressed in bold cubic forms, sparked immediate interest amongst Sydneysiders. Awarded the Sulman Medal in 1951(a prestigious New South Wales architectural prize) Seidler began receiving requests to design other peoples' homes and decided to stay in Australia indefinitely.

Focussing primarily on domestic architecture throughout the 1950s, the 1960s saw increasingly larger commissions starting with Blues Point Tower in 1961.

Founded in 1960 Harry Seidler and Associates went on to transform Sydney's CBD, constructing some of the city's most iconic buildings and re-shaping its urban spaces. Projects such as Australia Square (1967) and the MLC Centre (1975) altered the way people interacted with the city and, although designed around a thoroughly Modernist methodology, exhibited elements of sculptural sensitivity and regional practicality that were often hallmarks of Seidlers work.

Harry Seidler died in 2006 however his firm continues to make its mark on the built environment under the stewardship of his wife, Penelope.

Jorn Utzon (1918-2008)

When the NSW Government launched a design competition for a new opera house in 1955 it received 233 submissions from 32 countries. The eventual winner was a relatively obscure Danish architect whose work to date had consisted mainly of domestic projects around Scandinavia.

The son of a naval architect, Jorn Utzon was born in Copenhagen, where, in 1937, he attended the Royal Danish Academy of Fine Arts. After graduating in 1942 he moved to Stockholm, Sweden and worked with various Modernist architects including Arne Jacobsen and Poul Henningsen. Utzon travelled extensively following the end of the Second World War, beginning with Europe then onto Morocco, the United States and Mexico, before returning to Copenhagen in 1950 to start his own studio.

Completing a number of small projects throughout the 1950s, including his own home in Hellebaek (inspired by the work of Frank Lloyd Wright), Utzon set off again in 1957, visiting China, Japan and India before arriving in Australia to work on his most ambitious project yet.

From the beginning Utzon and his team were under enormous pressure from the state government to complete construction as early as possible. The state government feared that public opinion may baulk at the costs involved. This created less than ideal circumstances for such a grand project, especially one as complex and unique as the Opera House.

In 1965 a new state government was voted in, one that was less than enthusiastic about the project.

The incoming Minister for Public Works, David Hughes, clashed with Utzon over administrative, design and cost issues, which eventually resulted in the architect's resignation and departure in February, 1966. The role was taken over by Government Architect Peter Hall who oversaw the completion of the structure including the interiors, although these were not done to Utzon's original designs.

Jorn Utzon never returned to Australia. He spent the following decades working primarily in Denmark, producing a variety of domestic and commercial buildings, all of which reflect the well-travelled architect's eclectic Modernist influences and cultural experiences.

During the 1990's, in an effort at reconciliation with Utzon, he was approached by the Sydney Opera House Trust with a request for his involvement in any future alterations to the building. In 2004 a room was rebuilt to an original design by the architect and named in his honour. The Utzon Room features natural timber and bare concrete finishes and is decorated with a colourful 14 metre tapestry of the architect's own design.

When Utzon was awarded architecture's highest honour, the Pritzker Architecture Prize, in 2003, the citation read: 'There is no doubt that the Sydney Opera House is his masterpiece. It is one of the great iconic buildings of the 20th century, an image of great beauty that has become known throughout the world – a symbol for not only a city, but a whole country and continent.'

GLOSSARY

Bays: The spaces between posts, columns, or buttresses in the length of a building

Brutalism: An architectural style that emerged in the 1950s utilising raw concrete ('beton brut' in French) as the building material of choice.

Colonnade: A repeating series of columns supporting an upper structure

Curtain wall: The outer covering, or facade, of a building that is non-structural. New advances in aluminium and glass technology during the 1950s enabled the lightweight glass curtain walls that are ubiquitous on commercial buildings of this era

Elliptical: Oval in shape

Facade: An exterior side of a building, usually, but not always, the front

Floorplate: A concrete slab that forms an individual floor of a skyscraper

Hi-Tech: Also known as Structural Expressionism, a late Modern architectural style that incorporates cutting edge construction technologies and materials. Such buildings often reveal internal structures and forms externally.

Mullion: The vertical structural element forming a division between units of windows.

Plaza: An open urban public space

Podium: A platform used to raise a structure

Ribbon Windows: A series of windows set side by side to form a continuous band horizontally across a facade

Setback: The distance that a building's frontage is located from the street line

Spandrel: In reference to modern, multi-storeyed buildings, an infill panel between the top of one window and the sill or base of the one above. On 1950s curtain wall designs the spandrel was often a pane of opaque coloured glass.

Terrazzo: A composite material used extensively during the 1950s and 60s in both domestic and commercial architecture as floor and wall surfacing. Originally invented by Venetian construction workers, terrazzo consists of marble, quartz, granite or glass chips combined with a binding agent. The mixture is either poured on site, then ground and polished or pre-fabricated as tiles which can be laid in the traditional manner.

Truss: A series of straight members joined together in triangular forms to provide structural support

SYDNEY TIMELINE
1945-1990

1945 The Sydney-Hobart yacht race is held for the first time. The winner is 'Rani'.

1947 Population of greater Sydney reaches 1,484,434.

1951 Waverley Council bans the bikini swimsuit on its beaches.

1954 A Telex (teleprinter exchange) service is introduced to the city.

1955 Six o'clock closing of hotels in NSW ends. Bars are allowed to open till 10pm.

1956 Channel TCN-9 Sydney launches Australia's first regular television service.

1958 Cahill Expressway is opened.

1961 Trams in Sydney stop running.

1964 Bernard 'Midget' Farrelly wins the World Surfing Championship at Manly beach.

1966 Jorn Utzon resigns as designer of the Sydney Opera House.

1971 Green Bans are first imposed on building development in Sydney to protect heritage buildings.

1973 Sydney Opera House opens.

1976 Nude bathing is allowed on two Sydney beaches.

1977 Australia's worst railway disaster occurs when a commuter train from the Blue Mountains crashes into a concrete bridge at Granville, Sydney; 83 people are killed and many injured by the falling bridge.

1984 Hyde Park Barracks are restored and converted to a museum of social history.

1988 The First Fleet re-enactment vessels arrive at Botany Bay as part of Australia's bicentennial celebrations.

1990 Opera singer Joan Sutherland gives the final performance of her career at the Sydney Opera House.

THE WALK

The Footpath Guide to Sydney Modern architecture takes approximately two hours to complete.